Mic

by Cl

ACKNOWLEDGMENTS

The author simply wishes to thank Rockstar Games for creating the best video game series ever made. With hundreds and hundreds of hours invested in their *Grand Theft Auto* games, Clark was ultimately inspired to create this novel. In no way whatsoever should this book be viewed as a negative perception of one of their many masterpieces.

Prologue

He was waiting. Waiting with not a lot else to do. He was staring into the darkness of the tunnel, eager for something to appear. A change in the pitch of the light. It was silent. Absolutely silent so that he would hear it before he saw it. Probably. The kettle was slowly boiling but he was making it worse by watching it. A sound echoed the underground. A tip-tapping which grew a little in volume until a woman appeared at the platform. She was waiting now also, but at the far end of the platform. Just as he was trying to distinguish her features, two tiny bright lights appeared like marbles in the tunnel. Their shimmer bounced off the tunnel wall as they increased in size until the shine became harsh on his eyes. The sound of the brake and the engine pierced his ears as the metro came to a screeching halt. Right next to him on the track. The doors slid open.

***

Chapter 1

Mike was just another average guy touching forty. Satisfied with his office job, his lukewarm marriage and his nearly empty packet of Marlboros. It had been a short day at the office and once he'd arrived home Sharon was nowhere to be seen. 'Probably out shopping somewhere' he thought, whilst inspecting the contents of the fridge. To tell the truth he was expecting the-other-half to have fixed him up a hot plate but Toby was the only one satisfying his hunger. Mike stared blankly at the dog slavering away at the dry, meaty chunks that filled his bowl.

'Perhaps she forgot about me,' thought Mike; although he was sure he had told her about his half day due to his Boss's birthday. The fridge inspection proved unsuccessful and to his knowledge there were no chips or pizzas shoved in the freezer. His only real option was a bowl of cornflakes, complemented by room temperature UHT milk. They were out of the fresh stuff.

"Why doesn't she keep this shit in the fridge too?" he said out-loud whilst checking out the ingredients.

Toby observed him with his classic 'Don't look at me' expression. Mike remembered the times when Toby was fun and interesting. The times he used to be full of energy and always wanting to play fetch in the garden. Nowadays he was just a lazy, lifeless ball of fur who only showed affection to the mother of the house.

Mike slumped into his worn-leather chair. He had fished out a spoon from the dishwasher and he began tucking into his soggy cereal, wishing the whole time that the fucking milk was cold; just like the rain which began to patter against the newly-fitted double glazing. Half-finished, barely satisfied, he put the bowl on the floor by his foot and reached over the chair to grab his cigarettes which he'd left on the table. Luckily his lighter was inside the box waiting for him because he really couldn't be arsed with the whole saga of finding a lighter right now.

Just as he was sparking up his after-eating fag, the front door swung open and through it stepped his wife. Sharon was the same height as Mike, had dirty blonde hair and gentle features. Her lips were a pale pink colour, and she had slight dimples in her cheeks when she smiled. She loved to shop for clothes, but had a fairly simplistic style which she followed through the seasons. Her career had always been inside schools, typically as a secretary, for she was tidy and highly organised.

"Honeeeeey," she called.

'So she did know I was home,' Mike thought, "Hey, you okay?"

"Great! I bought some new- ... wait, what are you doing?"

"What do you mean?" he grunted.

"Smoking inside the house. Sitting in that damned chair of yours!" Her countenance had changed from one of happiness to one of irritation. She sighed. "I thought we spoke about this Mike? I thought we spoke about smoking indoors?"

"We did," he replied, "but like I said last time it's not like we have little kiddies running around and it's only an occasional habit."

"Hmmph" Sharon responded.

It was that noise she made whenever she felt flabbergasted at something Mike had said out-of-line.

"Occasional" she repeated, arms half folded still clutching her purchases. "Habit," she muttered (loud enough for him to hear) whilst pacing aimlessly around the living room amongst the smoky fumes.

Mike took one long final drag, and although it was only half-finished, he stubbed the rest out in the cereal bowl he left by his foot. The yellowish milk defused the tar-filled ash.

Sharon couldn't believe her own eyes. He knew it had pissed her off but he was armed and ready for his defence.

"What the hell are you playing at Mike? I mean-" she was angry now, "what the actual fuck?"

"Well you threw out the old ashtray so what am I supposed to do?"

She was about to scream at him "SMOKE OUTSIDE" but before she could do so he continued with his defiant stand.

"Besides, where is all the fucking food in this house and why do you insist on keeping that UHT shit out of the fridge? It's warm and disgusting!"

Mike looked at his wife, she was just shaking her head uncontrollably, totally in shock.

"You're disgusting Mike. Your attitude is awful these days!" She slammed the front door behind her and without telling him anything, she was gone.

Mike looked straight towards Toby who was giving him that look again.

Chapter 2

The stale smell of the stubbed out cigarette lingered in the living-room and had begun to drift up the stairs to the bathroom. The house was silent, a sharp comparison to the noise levels of only two minutes prior.
Emotion mastered reason, and Mike didn't feel sorry for standing up for himself. It's true that he loved Sharon, and he knew she always had his best interests at heart, but sometimes she could be such a fucking nag. 'I mean what's one cigarette sat on my chair in my house after a half-day?' he thought.

The rain had increased in volume since she had left the smoky living-room with her new shoes and dress; both of which she never got to show her husband. Mike moved from room to room inside the house, gazing blankly through the water droplets which were slowly dragging themselves down the window panes.
These underlying feelings of boredom and melancholy were becoming a regular occurrence within his mind. He was just thinking back to his early twenties, when times were great; when he was first dating Sharon and they used to go to the cinema together to watch a film, taking it in turns to choose each film whilst the other chose the restaurant.

'Maybe a night out is what I need' he kept thinking. One big blowout with all the lads for old times sake. 'Those were the days' he thought.
The football weekends with the boys down at the local on a Saturday. Back when you could have a cigarette and four or five pints and nobody was going to give you a hard time for it. Back when they all used to jump in the bookies to place

an accumulator on the league results, and with every goal a twist and turn in the tale.

The house phone started to ring and it took Mike by surprise. Everyone just called him on his mobile these days. The only people who ever rung the house phone were Sharon's dad or her sister Steph. Mike could never understand why Steph didn't ring her on her mobile like every other normal person. Then again there were a lot of things Mike didn't understand.

"Hello, who is it please?" he said as he picked up the phone sharply.

"Oh hiya mate it's me ’ows it goin’?"

“Chris?"

"Yeah man you got it in one, what's it been now hey? Fuck. A few years?"

"I guess it has Chris" Mike said, feeling a touch of guilt as to why he hadn't had the effort to stay in touch with the man who always used to be his close mate back in school.

"Yeah well you know 'ow it is don't ya? All this technology and all this accessibility and all tha’, but it's almost like it's even 'arder to stay in touch than it was before innit!?"

"I guess you're right yeah. What's up anyway how is it going with you? Same flat?"

"Nahh I 'ad to move a few months back. Kept gettin’ behind on my bill payments and I guess the landlord ’ad just ’ad enough kinda thing.”

"Ahh shit" said Mike, wondering what was Chris' motive here. Did he need money or something?

"Listen, mate I'm sorry to bother you and all that seriously. Are you busy?"

"I'm off my feet mate" Mike laughed. “No, I'm on a half day from the office. Can I help you out? What's up?"

"I'll cut to the fuckin' chase mate. I feel like a cunt for askin' ya but it's only 'cause I'm desperate. I'm pretty broke. I was thinkin'. You don't wanna buy my PlayStation off me for a bit do ya? I know we used to play it a lot when we were younger and that and you're a fuckin' grown man now and all tha' but the truth is I don't wanna sell it to someone I can't buy it back from when I get the money situation back sorted. D'ya get me?"

"Erm..." delayed Mike as his mind started to go haywire. What the fuck was this phone call about and where did it even come from? Why was he calling him on the house phone? What about the games console?

"Yeah why not how much do you want for it?" Mike said, figuring it could be a short-term cure for his boredom.

"Just give us one-fifty for it if ya want? It's the newest model like. Graphics are proper on it."

Mike felt the need to reinforce the deal, "Yeah alright yeah and then when you have the money again you can buy it back for the same price. Almost like a loan kind of thing if you like?"

"Sorted Mike I appreciate it I really do. I'll be over on my bike later on this evening. I'll bring all the cables and stuff with me."

"No problem" said Mike. "Look after yourself."

Chapter 3

Mr Hardy was two years younger than Mike and extremely well-kempt. You could always catch him in his office, clicking his pen and stroking his thin, trim beard. Mr Hardy was one of those new-age kind of bosses who always wore a skinny tie and made everyone feel like they were just another member of the team. The reality, Mike knew, was that Hardy fancied himself as the sharpshooting, highly effective executive who knew how to man-manage.

"Oh he does look handsome today doesn't he Carol?" said Babs,

"Well....I suppose" agreed Carol.

"I say, I don't know what it is about him but he sure knows how to work a suit," continued Babs, all in a fluster.

"Our Joseph bought his first suit at the weekend you know!"

"Oh aye? How old is he now love?"

"He's fifteen Babs. He's all grown-up now. I really don't know where all the years have gone?"

"In this place Caz, in this bloody place - ahhahahahahaha"

Mike could hear that grating loud laugh of Barbara's. That same laugh which he had endured for a few years now. That very laugh which kept him awake at night when his mind was wandering. He had a habit of doing that. Thinking back over the office at the things which generally annoyed him throughout the day. Thinking about those grey and blue walls, all the noises the computers made, and those small windows which didn't allow much light to pass through. Mike was happy that his office space was situated next to Kevin's. Quiet Kev. There was nothing particularly in common between himself and his co-worker but Mike appreciated Kev's "just get on with it" attitude.

Kevin was the kind of man who wouldn't speak unless spoken to. A little socially awkward if you like, but thoroughly likeable at the same time. Without a doubt there was something odd about him. His glasses were outdated, his ties were a bit drab and he had this weird *Ghostbusters* mouse mat which had faded in colour over the few decades since it had been manufactured. All day every day Kevin would tip-tap away on his greasy keyboard and very occasionally, Mike would catch him playing some strange game involving monsters and a village or something. Mike never asked questions and never made a fuss of it because he himself would procrastinate throughout the day, surfing the internet, checking his social media page or occasionally checking out the football results which he no longer really cared about.

Babs and Carol's office relationship couldn't be further from Mike and Kev's. Babs would natter away to Carol all day about celebrity gossip or the weather or Mr Hardy or about men in general. Her huge breasts almost annoyed Mike more than her bad jokes. They bounced around willingly and they were so hard to not look at sometimes. What Mike found awkward was that he was pretty sure Babs thought he liked them (and henceforth her), but the reality was that they were merely an office focal point. The elephants in the room.

"How's it going champ?"

It was Hardy, who had somehow sneaked up on Mike and given him that patronising thump on the back which men do to one another to exert status.

"Not bad Boss" replied Mike.

"Not bad also means not good though hey?" said Hardy as he winked and smiled at Mike.

"Aren't you going to congratulate me on the big Three-Eight Mike?" continued his Boss.
"Happy Birthday for yesterday. Thanks for giving us the half-day Boss."
"Oh Mike you know me. Treat others as you would want to be treated and all that, right? Right buddy?"
Mr Hardy gave him another pat on the back and casually walked off towards the desks of the women. Mike fucking hated Hardy.

Chapter 4

As a matter of fact, there were two other people who Mike hated *more* than Hardy. Firstly there was his flashy brother-in-law Tony, who made a thing of one-upping everyone. Then there was Ian. Big fucking annoying Ian who was the fifth and final member of Mr Hardy's "team". If "office-pet" is a term Mike thought, then Ian was exactly that. The way he bragged to Hardy and the rest of the office was borderline embarrassing, and it seemed to happen a lot of the time because his sales numbers were always the strongest.

Ian's desk was the closest in proximity to Hardy's office. In the opposite corner of the room to Mike and Kevin's and parallel to Barbara's and Carol's.
"Eeeeaaaassyyy tiger" he said to Babs as he swaggered over to their desks with a mug of coffee in his hand.
"How are my two gorgeous girls doing today?"
"Oh Ian what are you like?" said Babs as she chuckled flirtatiously.
"Working hard or hardly working Caz?"
"Working hard as always Ian" replied Carol honestly.
Ian would always do this. He would alternate his questions and eye contact between the two women to keep them both interested in him. Ian was one of those men who would pretend to show interest in others, when in reality it always came back to him. Mike could read him like a book.

It was at this moment that Mike realised Ian was using his mug. As a matter of fact he had washed it himself an hour earlier when he arrived to the office. Ian was always fucking late, but this was taking the piss. Mike had only just thought about making himself a coffee and now big, smug Ian was slurping from it.

Mike got out of his seat and was about to start walking over but Ian had just turned and moved towards Mike and Kevin's desks.
"Howdy partners, how are we both?"
"Not bad, we were just thinking about putting the kettle on, weren't we Kev?"
Mike included Kevin into the situation without even notifying him. Kevin was fine with it, but a little stumped as to why, seem as though Mike never normally spoke for the two of them.
"Oh is that so?" Ian replied. "I was actually going to ask you guys if you wanted one...but we only had enough milk for one"
"But I bought some semi-skimmed yesterday" said Kev a little awkwardly.
"Really?" said Ian, acting surprised.
"Yeah really," said Mike, "I saw him bring it back into the office and besides, why are you using my mug?"
Ian lifted up the mug to look at it properly, pretending to not know it wasn't his.
"This is yours?"
"Obviously pal. It has a big capital M on the front of it" Mike said with a degree of confidence.
Ian drew his face closer to Mike's and his expression became more serious. His tone became sharp.
"Listen Mike, it's just a fucking coffee cup okay!? Don't get smart with me or I'll embarrass you." Ian straightened up his posture, brought a smile back to his face and walked off over to his desk. He reached down to turn his computer on and put the M mug next to his mouse.
"I've never liked that guy" Kev said to Mike.
"Now you're talking my language Kev. To put it bluntly, the guy is a dick"

"Agreed."
This was a strange day for Mike and Kev's relationship. They never exchanged such small talk.

Chapter 5

Once Mike arrived home from work there was a plastic CD wallet on the floor. It contained a disc and a folded piece of lined-paper, which read as follows:

Mike,
Thanks again for taking the PS off my hands for a little while. Sorry for not giving you a fuckin game to play on. Found this copy of GTA down the side of my sofa. There are a few scratches on it but it should work fine like. I will buy the whole thing back off you v soon. I just need some time,
Chris

In some ways Chris had changed a lot but in other ways he was still the same old Chrissy. He was always the type to leave things lying around in odd places and he had never really been good with money. Although Mike was only judging from a phone call and a scrawled piece of folded paper, in his mind there was now a certain wiseness about his old friend. Perhaps due to acceptance?
In all honesty though, Mike was glad to have helped out a friend in need. It made him feel good about himself and his moral values. It was something with meaning which was important to a man who he thought lived a dwindling and meagre existence.

Mike scrunched up the letter in his hand, not angrily rather unknowingly, and then he tossed it towards the kitchen bin. It missed by about a foot and as Mike rolled his sea-green eyes his peripheral caught the disc, which was still inside the wallet which he still held in his left hand. The image depicted an attractive brunette woman blowing a kiss at him. Her visible earring, her bracelet and her ring (all on her right side) were gold, and she had a couple of tattoos. Her posture consisted of her bending forward slightly so that her large firm breasts were pushed together. She was inviting.

Mike had popped out to buy fags when Sharon got home. She ran a bath, poured some lotions and potions inside the hot, rising water and then she relaxed with her copy of *Pride & Prejudice & Zombies.* Mike could feel the distance between himself and his wife and had in fact been thinking about this very thing on the walk back from the petrol station. Pathetic or not, that walk back home in the dark smoking on his first cigarette straight from the packet was one of his favourite moments of the week. Alone time. Just him and his thoughts.

'I'm going to play that fucking game tonight when Sharon goes to bed -- it's not like she doesn't have her book -- and I swear I've not played a video game in at least ten or fifteen years! -- well, y'know, the odd game of FIFA against a mate.' He was thinking about a full game though. Classic single player. The PlayStation had been sitting in the corner of the living room for a few days now and Mike had never been bothered to tell Chris that he had forgotten to give him a game. Now he had the game, all he had to do was wait for the-other-half to hit the hay, put the kettle on for a brew, and that was that.

Chapter 6

As the kettle was boiling, Mike's thoughts drifted back to his last experience of playing *GTA.* The year was 2002, the in-game year 1986, the city was based around the sun-bleached backdrops of Miami. The *Carlito's Way* type lawyer, the motorbikes, the boats and Diaz's *Scarface* mansion.

'What a game that was!' Not forgetting that annoying as fuck mission where you had to pilot that remote control helicopter around a construction site for that old cowboy geezer.

Mike was ready. The kettle had clicked and he poured the scalding hot water from the spout into the mug until it infused with the tea leaves trapped inside their little flimsy bag. As he stirred the teaspoon and added a dash of milk, his eyes became transfixed with the copper and cream colours merging into one another, like two clouds revolving into a dusk-lit sky. Slowly the colours became one, a golden brown perfection to which sugar would only have ruined. Mike was not a big reader like his nephew Rich, in fact, he much preferred cinema and quality TV Series, but he had one time read this incredibly witty essay on how to make *A Nice Cup of Tea*. In it, Mike remembered that the author had distinctly said that addition of sugar was completely unnecessary, and would in fact destroy the savoury taste of the classic British brew.

Sharon was asleep upstairs, Toby was snoozing in his bed, and the digital alarm clock on the kitchen counter read 02:00.

'Funny' Mike thought, because recently he had been caught up in the habit of always looking at the time when it was precise to the hour. It was never a minute or so after or before. It just so happened that the last time he had a look at the time it was two o'clock also, but that was back in the office. Clock watching had become one of Mike's favourite past-times. The PlayStation had no troubles turning on once he plugged it in. The HDMi cable went smoothly into the back of the TV and the little bright red light on the black machine turned to a neon blue as he pushed the power button. The disc was still inside the plastic wallet and had been left on the dining room table which was just behind Mike's worn-leather chair. As he removed the disc he took one last look at the inviting woman, checked the bottom for scratches (of which there were a couple) and then inserted the disc into Chris' console.

Time stood still for the following few hours. Mike had been plunged into action. Thrown-in at the deep end. Some sort of bank heist job gone wrong in a snowy US town right off the beaten track. The graphics were way beyond anything he had been used to. Vivid in a way which he thought unimaginable. The digital alarm now read 04:14 which was an indicator that it was probably time for him to hit the hay. Besides, it was the weekend now and they had plans to visit Sharon's sister in the morning. Mike saved the game via his in-game mobile, turned off the machines and started heading up the creaky stairs to join his wife in their bed. As he clambered into bed as quietly as he could, his mind was still so active from all the flashing images of the television screen. His last memorable thoughts were about how thin the line had become between video-games and cinema.

Derailed

I can talk to you in confidence, right Doc?

Sure you can Michael. All your truths and all your lies will remain between the two of us. Right here in this room.

Oh that's reassuring, thanks Doc.

Not at all Michael, it's nothing. In fact, rather than your mental health therapist I want you to think of me as more of, just, a listener. Or, perhaps, your life guide. Keeping you on the right track sort of thing.

Might be a little late for that to be honest Doc. This train derailed years ago...

There's always time to re-correct past mistakes.

Is there? I mean, what if it's the case that *I'm* the mistake?

You are what you are Michael. A collection of acquisitions and experiences. You don't *choose* to make mistakes do you? I mean, purposely?

I guess not, but, does anyone? What I think I'm trying to say is that … I’m a fucking prick.

You have a lot of things Michael. A lot of desirable things. A beautiful house, a loving wife, two children, money in the bank, and from the looks of it, quite a nice sports car.

But...

But, let me finish, you also have another thing it seems. You possess an insatiable thirst for happiness.

Doesn't everyone?

Some more so than others. Believe me!

Chapter 7

It was ten o'clock exactly when Mike woke up. His left eye was the first to open and it peered at the bedside analogue. Sharon was downstairs, fully dressed and more-or-less ready to go.

"Miiiiiike" she shouted from the bottom of the stairs, "when are you getting uuuuuup?"

Was it that extended vowel sound Sharon was using, the idea of visiting his sister-in-law, or just his lack of sleep that was making Mike so irritable? Probably a concoction of the three he thought as he threw back the white duvet cover and swung his legs out of the side of the bed and onto the carpeted floor.

"Miiiiiiiike how long is it going to take you to get ready?" shouted Sharon again,

"I am up now. Just about to brush my teeth. I will be ready soon!"

He was still half asleep, rotating his brush in small circles so that the white froth was building up, fizzing on top of his yellowish teeth. His eyes stared vacantly into the mirror in front of him, so that he almost stared through himself. Like he wasn't even looking at anyone.

Now and then his mind focused back on his teeth, but mentally, he was in and out of his dream-world, his bathroom and his playground of last night's gaming session.

"Come on Mike honey" said his wife as she walked into their bedroom which was adjacent to the bathroom. "Oh I am so excited to go shopping with Steph and catch-up with all the goss"

"Yeah I bet" responded Mike as he put his toothbrush down on the sink and walked back out of the ensuite to get dressed.
"You could do with a shave baby" she said after giving him a peck on the cheek. It didn't matter so much that they hadn't discussed their argument from the other day. Their love was undying.
"What time did you come to bed last night Mike I swear it was late! I bet you're still half-asleep aren't you?"
"Something like that" he said as he pulled on his white socks. "What is Tony's plan for the day?" Mike asked; hoping and praying to the good lord that he was busy doing something.
"I don't know Mike, Steph didn't say, but I'm sure Rich will be home so you can talk to him"
"Yeah I like Richie" said Mike; and he really did like Rich. Rich was artistic and creative in a way Mike always wished he'd been. Rich, although only eighteen, was cool in that none-cool kind of way. Not your typical popular kid, but well-read, naturally quite intelligent and he never got too hung-up on his appearance. Unlike his parents.
"I know she is your sister and I think Rich is a great kid but for god sake when will Tony realise he is just a giant dick that the world doesn't need?"
"Don't say that Mike! I know Tony can be quite... flashy, shall we say? But he's a good father to Rich and he takes care of my sister."
"Yeah but why does he try and one-up everyone all the time?" Mike replied. "Do you think he has a tiny cock and he's trying to make up for it?"
Sharon chuckled. It was the first time her husband had made her laugh in a few weeks.

Mike pulled up onto the kerb outside Tony and Steph's place. It was a humble little semi-detached, with a very pretty front garden full of different coloured flowers. Steph was a big fan of gardening, or at least she had been over this past year or so.

"I'm just going to have a fag before we go in" said Mike as he wound down his window.

"Okay honey I am going to go and knock on for them," she kissed him on the cheek, undid her seatbelt and got out of the car. As Sharon walked up the garden path, Mike slipped a straight cigarette out of his box, lit it up and assessed the situation at hand.

Steph opened the door with a huge, beautiful smile on her face. Steph was sexy, there was no doubt about it. Her body was trim and her hair was always perfect. Apart from when they occasionally went out for a nice meal all together, Mike never ever saw Steph wearing anything but gym clothes. Gym clothes around the house, gym clothes going for a jog, gym clothes in the supermarket, gym clothes in bed more-than-likely.

He finished off his cig, undid his seatbelt and wound up the car window. It wasn't right for him to think about Sharon's sister in a sexual manner. Those were naughty thoughts he could get in trouble for if he ever revealed them.

There he was. Tony had appeared at the front door now.

"Mikey Boyyy!" he said in that flashy-father manner.

"Hey what's going on man?" Mike replied normally,

"Not much at all maaan. Honestly not much at all. I mean, there is this one thing that's pretty sw- naaahhh I'm just fucking with ya," said Tony whilst slapping Mike on his shoulder.

The sisters were already inside the house talking frantically, catching up about lots of important things.

Mike was conscious of his proximity in relation to Tony. He didn't like him *that* much that he wanted to be at a distance to him at all times.
"Is Richie in?" Mike questioned,
"Yeah he's upstairs in his room like *always"*
'Is he putting on a slight American accent?' Mike thought. 'If he is, that is fucking pathetic. Who does he think he is?'
"Anyway maan what's happening with you? You good? You good buddy?"
"Yeah I'm not bad honestly. Works as always. Same old same old"
"Yeah I can totally relate. I can totally relate-"
"I'm sorry can I just use your bathroom I'm kinda dying.."
"Of courrrse. It's just up the stairs on the right next to the boys room"
"Cheers" said Mike heading straight towards the stairs which were pretty well polished for some reason, to a level which almost made them dangerous. Mike hated a fall.
"Who's that?" came a voice from a room which the door was almost closed. A red light tinged through the crack and the atmosphere was generally a little darker to the rest of the well lit and well decorated house.

Chapter 8

"Oh hiya Uncle Mike, nice to see you. I figured it would just be Auntie Sharon" said a cross-legged Rich from his double bed.
"You figured wrong buddyyy" Mike replied, imitating Rich's father.
"Stop that right now. Jesus, Mum and Dad are both doing my head in. They are always on my case and I'm pretty sure they don't understand me at all."
Mike wandered slowly around Rich's room, surveying the posters on the walls and the various action figures stood in different poses. There was a classic yellow-and-black Wolverine with unsheathed claws, a T-1000 from *Terminator 2* and a Han Solo in carbonite, all in different places.
"Cool figures" said Mike honestly.
"Thanks. Big Ton' downstairs thinks they are, as he puts it, sad."
"Fuck him what does he know!?" Mike responded without thinking. It was the kind of comment he could get away with to Kev at work, but not at Tony's own son.
"Yeah ... I guess" said Rich. "All he ever seems to do these days is go to the gym. Or talk about the gym. Or say overtly sexual things to Mum which is kind of embarrassing but, you know - that's Dad!"

Mike was already tired of talking about his brother-in-law, and for a moment felt a little awkward just standing there, hands in pockets, afraid to tell a secret.
"What's new with you anyway Uncle Mike?" questioned Rich intriguingly,
"You know how it is as an adult. Same shit, different day" retorted Mike.

"You sound like-"
"But," Mike interrupted, "I was actually playing this game last night which I bet you like"
"What kind of game?" asked Rich, thinking he might be meaning a card game or possibly even a drinking game.
"Well an old friend of mine kind of lent me his PlayStation and a copy of *GTA*."
Rich's eyes lit up, his body animated.
"The new one?"
"*GTA*? Yeah I think so" replied Mike.
"No I meant the console Uncle Mike"
"Yeah, it's the latest one, at least I'm pretty sure it is. I haven't played a *GTA* game in years and years though. Fuck-ing hell the graphics these days!"
"Crazy aren't they!? I fucking love Rockstar Games man. They did an old western on the last-gen consoles and I got 100% on that shit!"
Rich was in such a good mood now. Just talking about video games with his Uncle.
"Where are you up to on it?"
Mike reached into last night's memory, to try and recount the details of the first mission which he completed in the early hours of the morning.
"Oh just the first mission. Out in the sticks with all that snow around. That bank heist with your two buddies. I was completely gripped"
"Yeah the gameplay is ridiculous isn't it."

There was a knock at the door.

"Did you get lost on the way to the bathroom bro? End up in the cave? Hahahaha" laughed Tony, slapping his hands against his own thighs.

"Do you have to call me 'Bro' all the time Ton'? I mean I know I'm technically your brother-in-law but you sound so American. You're British!"
Mike was talking with a rare confidence his nephew had never really heard before. It was quite refreshing.

Chapter 9

Mike's alarm sounded at 07:30, but he added another twenty minutes onto it for a ten-to-eight official wake up. Now, twenty minutes is a strange amount of time when one is still so tired from the night's sleep, and this particular twenty minutes was just enough time for Mike to slip into a vivid dream. It started by looking down at a teaspoon swirling in a circular motion around a cup of tea. The ripples, bubbles and steam intertwined with one another, emitting a bittersweet smell. Time was distorted within time and Mike jumped into the scene of the crime.

The hostages were face down on the floor, hands behind the back of their heads. They were shouting something inaudible. Red lights from the alarm system disorientated the situation, but Mike was comfortable.

His two American companions kept shouting instructions through the holes in their balaclavas and next thing they were all out in the crisp snow, their boots crunching imprints into the ground with every pressing step. A bag of money was hanging over his left shoulder and he gripped an M4 assault rifle to help fight back against the barrage of bullets which kept flying past his head.

Ergh ergh ergh ergh ergh

Mike slammed his hand down on the bedside alarm clock. Sharon was already downstairs, making breakfast and jotting down notes in her organiser. In just his boxers, he clambered out of the bed and headed straight to the bathroom to empty his bursting bladder and jump in the shower. For whatever reason Toby was sat in the centre of the bathroom floor looking sorry for himself, which Mike

took as an easy opportunity to vent some of his "late for work" grumpiness.
"Fucking move you miserable old dog" he said as he nudged Toby with his bare foot.
As the shower water reached its optimum temperature, Mike's sleepy brain was transfixed on the vividity of his dream, and a nice cup of tea.

He left his damp towel on the bed, pulled on his white shirt and twisted a knot in the first tie he had grabbed from the wardrobe and flung around his neck.
"Those work shoes could do with a quick clean love" said Sharon as Mike galloped down the stairs.
'Not now' Mike thought, "Yeah" he replied, just before giving his wife the routine morning peck on the cheek.

As he reached to the top cupboard to grab the box of cereal, Sharon was looking at something on his persons. She had one of those disapproving looks on her face,
"Oh Mike, how many times have I told you now? That friggin' shirt is going yellow under the arms!"
"This milk's going yellow n'all," he replied nonchalantly, "when did you buy it?"
Sharon hated it when her husband undermined her.
"Last week. Remember? You were complaining!"
Mike wasn't fully registering what she was saying, he was too preoccupied with being late for work. So he finished up his cereal, grabbed his keys and his pack of fags, and opened the front door.
Just as the door was about to close behind him, Sharon shouted,
"Did you drape the towel over the radiator?"
But it was too late. The door slammed. He was gone...

Chapter 10

He was definitely going to be late. Hardy would no doubt be a twat about it, and Babs would have something to gossip about all day with Carol. He was sitting at the last set of traffic lights just before the left turn he needed to take. Of course it was on red, which had seemed to set like Mike's mind heading back into sleep mode. He was so fucking tired all the time these days. Days dragged into one another so frustratingly. It was a fairly nice day outside though. The sun was creeping through the white clouds and a gentle breeze came through the gap in the door window.

A man in faded powder blue jeans wearing a big pair of Oakley sunglasses sprung out of the door of the bookies which was to Mike's right over the other side of the road. As the man took off his shades Mike recognised him. It was his stupid brother-in-law staring at his smart-phone with a big grin on his face. Mike looked back to the light but it was still red. So he shuffled down a little bit into his seat to lower the sight of his head. Just in case Tony caught a glimpse of him and started doing something garish and embarrassing as always.

Still red. It was now somehow 09:13 and Mike thought back to being late. Finally green, he over-revved the engine a little and span his sedan around the corner. Tony looked back due to the noise but to him it was just another dark green car. He went straight back to his mobile phone.

The air-conditioning system at the office was broken. The atmosphere was sticky when Mike arrived.

"Hey hot shot where have you been buddy?" Hardy asked as Mike headed towards his desk. He could see Kev tip tapping away on his greasy keyboard and he was momentarily jealous of him. Mike was still in that sleepy

state and it was the clicking and unclicking of Hardy's ballpoint which brought him back into the scene.
"I'm really sorry but there were just a few complications this morning that's all."
"Hmmm I bet" replied Hardy. It was one of his empty yet suggestive responses, which typically left an awkwardness lingering in the air.
"Anyway I best get to it Boss"
"Yeah I'd say that's a good idea Mike."
He looked at the pen which Mr Hardy was still clicking, and then he walked off to his desk, ignoring the rest of the office.
"Morning Kev how's it going?"
"Oh hi Mike not bad. Well, except it's pretty stuffy in here."
It was stuffy. It made Mike irritable but at the same time, he was just thinking about how much he appreciated Kev. After all these years, after all the times Mike had bitched about him to his mates in the pub, there was something so carefree and relaxed about his geeky co-worker. To put it bluntly, Kev never gave Mike any shit; and for this he was glad.
"Where's the dickhead this morning?" asked Mike, referring to Ian.
"Where do you think?" replied Kev, "Licking Hardy's balls as per usual."
Mike laughed, and it was then he saw Hardy receiving a mug of tea from Ian. The pair of them were chatting away about sales figures and the weeks projections. A very different conversation to the one Mike had just had with his Boss.
'God he's so detestable' thought Mike.

Chapter 11

"I don't know when she'll be here Carol"
"I hope she's nice Babs"
"Oh won't it be so lovely to have another woman in the office with us! I'm tired of all these *men"*
"Tell me about it babes."
It was incredible how a private conversation between two colleagues could be heard so easily around the office. Carol was usually the listener and Babs the loud-mouth, but it was as though Babs' bad habit had projected itself onto quiet Carol, and now the pair of them were just another set of gossips.
Mike leaned his head round to speak to Kev, who was working hard as always, but with the same lethargic nature he had adopted over the last few months.
"Hey Kev" said Mike, "is there a new girl starting in the office?"
"First I've heard of it."
It's true that Mike had never really viewed Kev as much of a ladies man. Not to knock him, but it was clear he preferred time alone with his PC or his comic collection.
Ian had made his way over to Mike and Kev's desk,
"What are you gentlemen talking about so secretly?"
Ian hated secrets unless they were his own to share.
"Nothing" replied Mike. It was always Mike who answered when a question was directed at his and Kevin's desks.
"Come on boys, do tell. It didn't look like nothing did it Kev?"
Ian had this awful habit of trying to gain comrades to support his views and opinions. He recruited through motions of discomfort.

Kev ignored him and continued to tap away on his greasy keyboard.
"Oi Kevin that's kinda rude innit!? HA, well I don't give a fuck about talking to you pair of puffs anyway. There's going to be a cheeky chica joining the ranks and it goes without saying that she's automatically mine" jaunted Ian, his dickhead high school mentality in full blossom.
"Oh of course Ian. I'm sure she loves guys pumped full of teen bravado" Mike remarked dryly.
Ian's face crimsoned. He was used to giving it out and that's all. He drew his angered head towards Mike's so that their noses were practically touching.
"You listen here Michael. Whether she is fit or not I doubt she's going to end up sucking your little prick."
And then just like that, Ian picked himself up, changed face and wandered over to Babs and Carol. As if nothing had happened.
"Ladies ladies ladies tell me everything"
"We don't know 'owt" replied Carol.
"Hasn't Hardy told you anything over your little tea breaks?" suggested Babs, smirking while she said it.
"Oh you're funny aren't you big tits!" said Ian, as Mike lost interest in eavesdropping.

Mike thought about what had happened earlier that day. When he'd seen that other prick in his life. His wanker of a brother-in-law. He wondered why he was surrounded by so many false personas. People with no status who thought they were the real deal. It was on his lunch break that he thought back to his game. He couldn't wait to get comfortable on his sofa, enjoy the last ends of his cigarette and get his teeth stuck into the story. That way he could talk to Rich about it in a bit more detail, whilst on another of his "toilet breaks".

Charlies

Tell me about *that* day Michael....

Well, it all took place in broad daylight would you believe!? I was sitting outside at this little cafe I like. Sipping on an iced coffee, the sun was beating down on the strip. I was wearing my Rays which I'd only bought the week before in Miami.

Right...

Oh and yeah, it was a good job I had them on because Doc, you wouldn't believe the women walking past me that day! Their vibrant bikinis, their sun kissed skin. Anyway, I'd been keeping my eye on Charlies for a few weeks. Just observing the cash flow, the clientele, the popular times, this and that this and that.

I understand. Do, please, continue.

You know when you've got that feeling?

What feeling Michael?

That urge. That irrational desire to just act in the moment.

You mean when a person chooses to almost ignore logic and reason, favouring impulse instead?

Something like that. Except things feel different after you've done time inside. I knew if I was going to do this it needed to be thorough. It needed to be calculated.

Anyway, I lit up a Cuban and continued to observe. The coffee had made me a little edgy and so I asked the waiter to bring me something a little stronger.

A Scotch perhaps?

Come on Doc! You know me by now don't you? Scotch for the nights and Bourbon for the daytime.

Neat and on the rocks?

There we go... But I'll cut to the chase. The time was around two-thirty and the doorman at Charlies had just set off on his usual post-lunch break. I gave my I.T. guy a call to temporarily disable the security system - which isn't the most high-tech, believe me - and then it was game on.

How exciting Michael!

Oh come on Doc, don't give me that high horse sarcasm crap.

I'm sorry. That's your job right?

Right. And so, I knocked back my bourbon, threw a twenty note on the table and crossed over the road. The sun bounced off the palm leaves. The sky shimmered it's perfect blue above me. The air was still. I grabbed the handle of my M9...

Beretta?

Always. They're the most trustworthy. And just as I pushed open the door, I pulled it out from my pants, gripped it with my right hand and supported it with my left. I told the bartender,
"Don't cause a FUCKING scene just open the register and put the money inside a holdall!"

My gosh. That must have been an intense moment Michael. But how did you know they had a holdall inside the bar? And how did you escape?

I'd seen a couple of tennis chumps enter for a post-match late lunch. Like I said, it was calculated. Anyway these two fuck heads were scared shitless. A few customers crouched down with their hands behind their heads but no-one screamed or anything. It was silent and seamless. No need for shots fired. Although I did have a fully loaded clip. The last thing I remember is fleeing the scene, running down the adjacent alleyway, my blood pumping and my heart beating like the ever-watching sun.

And do you remember how much you got away with?

Of course Doc. I remember more or less every score. The greatest thing about Charlies Bar is they only deposit the cash on a weekly basis rather than daily like most other bars. If I remember rightly this particular score was about eight thousand dollars.

Chapter 12

Mike got stuck in traffic on the way home too. It pissed him off that not only was he working the mundane nine-to-five, his day seemed to always be extended staring through his car windows at the drizzle.

Once he arrived through the front door, the distinct smell of cottage pie whiffed against his nose.

"Hi honey are you okay? How was work today? Tea's nearly ready!"

"Yeah it wasn't too bad. Ian's still a twat"

"Well, you know. Some people never change honey"

'That's true' thought her husband.

Sharon was so good to Mike. Yes she could be irritable at times, but that was marriage for you. In general, she was a happy person. Clean, honest and organised.

"You know I spent the day with our Steph today. We went for a quick look around the shops and she was telling me about this couples membership at the gym that her and Tony have. It's a great offer you know!"

"Oh yeah?" replied Mike despondently, kicking off his work shoes and slumping into his chestnut leather chair. He closed his eyes and knocked his head back.

"It's only fifty-two fifty a month for the pair of us, but I know it'll take a miracle to get you to the gym!" said Sharon as she divided the dinner into six perfectly equal portions.

"I'll think about it love." Mike's mind was elsewhere. *GTA*, the new mystery colleague, his sighting of Tony earlier that day and even his old friend Chris.

"Oh and Rich asked about you too. That was nice of him wasn't it!"

"Oh yeah what did he want?" Mike asked opening his eyes.

"No idea give him a call if you like hon'".

Once dinner had settled Mike loaded the dishwasher. The clouds had drifted apart outside unveiling a dark blue tinted sky. The kitchen clock read 20:13 and Sharon went upstairs for a bath. It was time to enter the disc and spend an hour or two on his game. The phone rang. Not his mobile but the home phone again which made Mike assume it was Steph. He couldn't be bothered with her gym spiel right now.

"Hello who is it please?" asked Mike as was custom when answering thc landline.

"Hey man guess who!?"

"Chris?"

"Spot on my man spot on. Listen 'ows the gaming goin' for ya?"

Chris was speaking with slightly broken fluency due to the fact that he was smoking a fag. It made Mike want one too. As a matter of fact it was Chrissy who first got Mike into smoking. Back in high school behind the hill by the old sports centre.

"It's funny you should ask actually mate," replied Mike, pleasantly surprised to be talking to his mate again and not an automated sales call or his sister-in-law; "I was just about to have a little session. I've only played the first little bit but fuck me it's great innit!"

Chris started laughing before he answered,

"What the game or the machine?"

"Both" Mike said checking his box of Marlboros, which, was predictably empty.

"Yeah the graphics are solid and that latest *GTA* is mega innit. How times 'ave changed since the *Vice City* days 'ey?"

"Yeah I know," Mike said, as small pangs of guilt began to rise in the pit of his stomach like acid bubbling gently. "What's up anyway? You aren't going to ask for it back just yet are you?" Mike laughed, "I'm becoming invested."
"Nah nah I 'aven't got the money together yet Mike. I was actually callin' to see if ya wanted to get together soon, for a smoke or a beer or somethin'?"
"Sure man. Sounds good."

It was quarter-to when Mike finally got back on the game. He did a couple of missions but was far too distracted with the sheer expanse of this sandbox world. Curtains closed to avoid more distractions, Mike took pride in controlling his protagonist. The high-definition colours shone through the television screen as he jacked cars, chased pedestrians and ignored traffic lights. He skidded stolen vehicles around wide open bends and casually flicked through a wide array of radio stations as the setting sun cast its peachy orange glow over the west coast landscape. This was true escapism. A world in which traffic jams didn't exist, in which you could ride a motorbike at top speeds with no helmet, and a world in which he could pull out a firearm on a police officer and press the trigger repeatedly.
All without consequence.

Chapter 13

Mike slept soundly that night; like a tired twelve year old at the end of a perfect birthday. He dreamt one of those dreams you can't remember the details of, so that he was half-convinced he didn't even dream. It was a perfect eight hour sleep which left him pleasantly refreshed. Mike was one of those typical adults who had left video-gaming in the past. He'd grown to accept that it was one of those hobbies left to kids and overgrown geeks like Kevin. But the truth was he had greatly enjoyed his evening alone with the PlayStation. His spirits were high and matched the weather outside where the morning sun was rising between the fluffy white clouds.

"I've made pancakes and coffee is on the side for you hon'" said Sharon as he pecked her on the cheek.

"Thanks baby" he said, sitting at the breakfast bar and sliding a knob of butter on top of his hot pancakes. Watching it melt poetically into their sweet centres.

"It's a lovely morning isn't it Mike? There have even been a few birds in the bird house. I think that robin is back from spring!"

"Are you not having any pancakes baby?" Mike asked.

"No no I'm watching my figure" she replied, as she took the butter and scraped it over her slice of brown toast. He'd never say anything, but Mike was convinced his wife was growing more jealous of her sisters lifestyle.

"You really don't need to Shaz; you know I love you just the way you are!"

"Aww that's sweet of you" she said, flicking open her organizer.

They left the house together that morning. Mike got into his green sedan and Sharon her yellow Fiat. Mike

started the engine and lowered his side window to let some fresh air into the car. The drive started smoothly and for some reason the roads weren't very busy. Mike thought about the contrast between the real world and *GTA* as one of the traffic lights turned to amber and he pulled to a stop. He couldn't just cruise straight through like his protagonist could. It was then, whilst waiting for the green light, that he heard a soft buzzing noise. He looked around the car to locate the fly when he was caught off guard by a louder buzz just past his left ear. The perpetrator was
an enormously large bumbling bee. He watched the yellow and black furry blob land on the inside of his front window, just underneath the rear-view mirror. Momentarily distracted by its unpredictability, he swiped the back of his hand towards it to try and shoo it away. A beep of a horn behind him caused him to jump which excited the bee further. His foot jerked on the clutch pedal which caused him to stall the car embarrassingly at the green light. Cars began to pile up behind him which forced more honks from impatient drivers.
"For fuck sake" he yelled, quickly starting up the engine again before over-revving and speeding off. By this time the bee had become frantic and was buzzing all around Mike's car like a crazed maniac debating murder.

By some miracle Mike arrived to the work car-park with five minutes to spare. His mood however, had changed, and his ankle had swollen to the size of a golf ball.
"Fucking little bastard" he exclaimed upon stretching the elastic of his sock to inspect the damage. The bee was lifeless upon the drivers car mat. Still as a widows house. Mike stamped on its corpse to make sure it really was the end of this force of nature. This honey suckler.

Terrible at ailments and out of proximity of any dock leaves, Mike craved a cigarette to iron out his stress levels. He was, of course, still out of fags. The only smokers in the office were Ian and Babs and he didn't feel like asking either; the former for obvious reasons and the latter because he wasn't in the mood for flirtatious banter and an earful.
As he approached the outside front door, Carol was on the phone to her son.
"Alright Joseph give me a call later and let me know how it goes sweetie.................alright then, bye now!"
"Morning Carol" said Mike as he hobbled through the car-park.
"Are you alright love?" she asked, showing some concern.
Mike hated it when any attention was drawn towards him.
"Fine thanks. Just a little bee sting on my ankle"
"Oh you poor thing I'll fetch you an antiseptic wipe from my handbag when we go up. Oh and remember, the new girl starts today!"

Chapter 14

Mike wasn't listening to Carol's news about her son's job interview but he acknowledged her as if he was. Their office was on the thirteenth floor which made for a long lift journey to and from the office and the ground floor. Mike switched his phone to silent and tried hard not to concentrate on the throbbing redness of his ankle. 'Why did my pleasant morning have to be ruined by a stupid insect' he thought. It was as if something was monitoring his levels of happiness, like an overly strict lifeguard at a kids swimming pool party.

"Now I've told the new girl to get here at ten today," announced a perfectly dressed Hardy once the six of them were all inside the confines of the office. "Reason being I wanted to make sure we make a good impression. I spoke to my seniors just this morning and they have informed me that if, for whatever reason, she isn't satisfied here, she will have the option to move up to floor fourteen."

As he spoke he was clicking his ballpoint, pacing the room slightly and smoothing his trim goatee. Barbara was transfixed on her boss like some sick puppy, whilst Carol was rummaging around for Mike's ailment.

"I've spent quite some time with her CV," continued Hardy, "and it's safe to say that she is more than, perhaps *over*-qualified for this job."

The comment stung Mike for a second time that morning.

"Now, she'll be situated next to Ian's desk so I shall be able to keep an eye on her from my office" Hardy exclaimed.

"Typical" Kev muttered to Mike, just as Mike spied an uncomfortable smile appearing on Ian's fucking face.

"But I want each and every one of you to make her feel welcome, and, most importantly, part of the team!"

Hardy was finished with his speech and was just about to head into his glass office space when Ian piped up,
"Do you want me to show her up to the office boss?"
"If you wish" Hardy replied, closing his door behind him.
"I hope she's fuckin' ugly" Mike whispered to Kev, who chuckled quite loudly before moving back to his computer.

As it turns out, she wasn't. Tina was the kind of woman who was naturally beautiful, but who never acknowledged it herself. Whether she recognised that others found her attractive is hard to tell, for she viewed herself as just another ordinary person, and valued herself on her career ambitions and her behaviour towards others. It was apparent from her short introduction that she was nervous, and from her accent that she was not from around these parts. Tina was extremely well dressed, as if prepared for an interview. She wore traditional black heels, tights, a pencil skirt, and on top a white frilled buttoned-up shirt with a smart grey blazer. Her skin was the colour of mocha cappuccino, her lips a voluptuous red and her hair curled perfectly like crests of Caribbean waves which shimmered in the light. There was nothing false about her, she was real in every sense of the word. Unlike Ian, who within seconds of arriving into the office with her had become a slimier snake than Mike thought possible.
"Jesus," Mike said to Kevin, "I wouldn't be surprised if he's already offered her a back rub!"
"Hah, yeah" was the only response he received. Kevin had never been the most expressive of people.
Barbara and Carol were excited by Tina's arrival. They tried to gossip less obviously, but Mike knew they couldn't wait to find out more details about her. Hardy called her into his office as to assert his pen-clicking authority, much to the

disappointment of Ian who was more than keen to portray his "alpha" status.

It was hard to pin an age on Tina thought Mike. 'Possibly early thirties' as he was certain she was the youngest, as well as the newest member of the team. Lost in the pensive thoughts of a married man, Carol interrupted with her kind gift which was to soothe his sore ankle.
"Here you are Mike love" she smiled.
"Oh, thanks Carol"
"Oh what are you like it's nothing. Our Joseph had a nasty bite just last week!"
Mike never knew what to say whenever Carol mentioned her child. Just like whenever Sharon would hint to him that she wanted to give it another try.

Chapter 15

It was time for a clean shave and a new white shirt. Sharon was right about the yellowing armpits. Mike had become hygienically lazy as of late, and although he hadn't had a chance to properly meet his new colleague on her first day at the job, he only felt it right that he should make a little effort. Thus, he woke earlier than usual on Saturday morning, with a busy day ahead of him. First he would shit, shave and shower. Then he would head to the shopping mall (picking up fags on the way), then he would pay a visit to his sister-in-laws and see Richie, and finally, at night, he was meeting Chris at the pub for a pint.

He left Sharon sleeping in bed that morning, pecking her on the cheek with his new smooth face. He'd even been a good husband and made sure to wash away all his tiny facial hairs from around the bathroom sink. Toby was downstairs alone when Mike prepared the cafetière. Mike gave him a little attention, tickling him under the chin, rubbing his belly and flapping his ears, but Toby continued his vacant stare.

"Are you hungry boy? Are you thirsty?" Mike asked before seeing Toby's two bowls full in the kitchen corner. A whimper was the only response he managed to get, before the dog slumped himself on the chestnut chair.

Mike filled his takeaway plastic flask with half of the hot coffee, and left the other half for his darling wife, who, at long last, had purchased fresh milk and had even put the UHT inside the fridge door. As he drove to the petrol station to fill up his sedan and purchase his Marlboros, his mind was on sex. It's true the honeymoon period doesn't last forever, and it's also true that most married couples don't fuck like rabbits, but it had been months now since

Mike and Sharon had last got it on. Perhaps it was time to take her out for a nice meal he thought. Wine and dine her then back home for some Luther Vandross and some passionate loving.
"A pack of Marlboros and a Snickers please" he said to the girl, who looked young, but had a pair of beautiful bright blue eyes.
"Any petrol today?" she asked customarily, as the pair locked eye contact briefly before she blushed ever so slightly.

There's always something that clicks after a man grooms his hair. A switch of electrical current. Mike rubbed his chin continuously as he sauntered around the mall. The girl at the petrol station wasn't the only attractive person he interacted with that day. He found himself unassumingly flirting with the shop assistant in the shirt shop, a woman with perfectly executed make-up at the fragrance counter, and even a girl in her twenties at the fast-order lane at McDonalds. What was up with him today? He wasn't too sure but it was refreshing like the new eu de toilette he had treated himself to. 'Exotica', with hints of spicy pineapple and creamy coconut.

On my way to your sisters. Meet you there. Mike x he text his wife. It was another sunny and cloudy day. Perfect for winding down the window and having a smoke whilst driving. It was a casual drive, and there wasn't much traffic on the roads. He was just finishing the last dregs of his cooled-down coffee when he spied Tony again, in more or less the same place as he had seen him last time, on the opposite side of the road coming out of the bookies. He couldn't help but see his brother-in-law, as he was wearing a garish pink polo shirt and his stupid big shades. Really, he should have pulled over to the side of the road, beeped his horn and offered him a lift. He didn't.

Once he arrived at Rich's house, both cars were on the driveway. Tony's and Steph's. Mike rang the doorbell and it was Steph who answered.

"Oh hi Mike love great to see you" she smiled, "where's Sha'?"

'God you look so sexy in those tight gym clothes' he thought,

"Oh we've come separate" he said, "I've been running a few errands"

'Must not look at those perfect tits, must not think about Steph this way' his mind instructed.

"Where's Tony? Is Richie in?"

"Ton' was at a friends last night. Poker night I think. First Friday of every month. Rich is upstairs in his room."

"Ah I see I see," answered Mike as he stepped through the front door, "do you mind if I pop up and see him?"

"Of course not love he always likes seeing you". There was something in her tone Mike couldn't put his finger on.

"Oh hey Uncle Mike" Richie beamed as he knocked and entered. Rich was sat up on his bed reading a book.

"What you reading there?"

"*East of Eden* by John Steinbeck. Have you read it? It's great!"

"No, no I haven't read that one. Only read Grapes but that must have been ten or so years ago now."

Mike sat down on the bed and stared at his nephews *Reservoir Dogs* poster on the wall. It was the classic walking shot of the colour-coded Mr's.

"They're both great novels but this one is a bit more religious" Rich said, "a bit more spiritual."

"I'll have to check it out. Steinbeck is one of the greats. Actually, it's fantastic you're reading such things at your age. I always found I got into reading too late" Mike said, a little jealous of Rich.
"Who's your favourite?" asked Rich, seeing his Uncle still cross-examining the poster.
"Not sure actually. I've always loved Blonde and Pink. Steve Buscemi is one of my favourite actors" said Uncle Mike.
"I love Mr White..." Rich was saying when he was interrupted by his Dad downstairs.
"I'm hooome sexy!" Tony announced, "Where are you I wanna slap your botty!?"
Rich closed his eyes in pain. Mike creased.
"Anyway how's *GTA* treating you Uncle Mike?"
"Oh really well. Honestly all credit to the developers the gameplay is incredible. I've not done too many missions I was just cruising around and having mad chases with the police the other day."
"Yeah that's the beauty of it" replied Richie, "you've got the freedom to do what you want!"
"Definitely. I love the way all the vehicles handle uniquely as well" said Mike, "honestly I don't know how they do it!"
The doorbell rang.
"That must be Sharon. I best go say hello...."

"Look at you honey" his wife smiled as he walked down the stairs to greet her. Tony was in the kitchen, busy snogging Steph and groping her bottom.
"Yeah I had a shave and popped to the mall for a few things" Mike said as he kissed her on the lips.
"You smell wonderful, what did you buy?" asked his wife, inhaling the sunny beach aroma.

"Heeey buddy you alright? How's it going Shazza?" Tony swaggered into the room with his arm around Steph.
"Not bad not bad, same old same old" Mike replied, reluctantly.

Chapter 16

Sharon was so delighted with her husbands decisions to freshen up, that she decided she wanted to go home and have sex. For she too was aware of the bedroom hiatus. It didn't take long for her to convince Mike to leave her sister's house and go home. It was around three o'clock when she whispered in his ear seductively, "I want you... let's go home".

"I've just remembered we forgot to put any water in Toby's bowl" Sharon told Steph, who looked a little disappointed that they were leaving so promptly on a Saturday.

"Not to worry 'ey!" said Tony, slapping Steph's bum whilst winking at Mike, "we've got a few things we have to do as well haven't we baby?"

The conversation on the way home consisted of Mike's morning, and the grotesqueness of Tony's behaviour.

"I feel sorry for Richie" Mike said.

"Has he said something to you?" Sharon replied, rubbing her hand on Mike's thigh.

"Not really. I mean he's told me he's uncomfortable with his Dad's overtly sexual expressions but aside from that, I just think he's a great kid who isn't fully appreciated."

"I guess" said Sharon, which was followed by a short silence. The wind found itself through the gap in the car window and caused Sharon's dyed blonde hair to blow in her face. She swept it away and said,

"Steph's concerned Mike. I think she thinks Tony has a gambling problem."

"It's a dangerous game" replied her husband whilst focusing on the road.

The sex was abrupt, taking place almost as soon as they got through the front door. Toby knew what they were

up to. He stared blankly as always, whilst lay down on the kitchen floor. A rush of excitement tingled down Sharon's legs as Mike reached his hands under her dotted skirt and whipped her knickers down to her ankles.
"Are we not going to the bedroom?" she asked.
"No" he said, as he cupped his warm hand over her vagina. 'He's never this sexually confident' thought Sharon, as she arched her head back letting her hair fall. She was still wearing her high heels which Mike liked, as he knew he could insert her without having to bend his knees. He pressed her against the hallway wall and undid the button of his jeans, ripping apart the fly zip. Sharon could smell the 'Exotica' and moaned breathlessly through her nose as he slid his hard penis inside her. He reached his arms around her front to grab both of her breasts, thrusting all the while as they both moaned synonymously. And then the climax. It didn't last long. They both peaked early, but they enjoyed it.

Mike ordered pizza for tea, and they sat facing each other at either end of the sofa with the box in the middle, gossiping like teenagers. Once finished, Sharon went upstairs for her bath and book time. Mike saw it as a glorious opportunity to have a quick go on his game, as the time was just half past six and he was meeting Chris at the pub at nine. The birds-eye view camera descended down on Mike's protagonist. He was lay down on his deckchair, poolside. Mike decided to go and change his clothes from loose shirt, shades, shorts and sandals to a smart powder blue suit with black business shoes. He had a gorgeous house. Decorated with love, and his options were endless in the LA playground. Play tennis, purchase weapons, take part in a street race, pick up a sleazy hooker in his convertible. Mike opted for a few story missions, which included a breaking and entering, a beating-up of a dodgy car dealer and a heroic paternal yacht party break up, which resulted in a high speed jet-ski chase with 9mm Uzi bullets speeding past his hero. Then he decided to go and see his therapist at his comfortable beach-house residence.

Home Safe

Talk to me about your relationship with women Michael. How are things with your wife?

Oh she's the same as always Doc. Giving me a hard time about the kids. Telling me that I smoke and drink too much. Out spending hundreds on the latest fashion labels.

I see I see. Would you describe her as, I don't know, "Materialistically Obsessed"?

I'm not sure Doc. Probably. Diamond's are a girls best friend, right? But anyway, I caught her in the garden the other day. Chatting to our neighbour, Hayden. He's this golf obsessed prick who lives alone. Probably jacking off every night in his patterned crew-knit. My wife was mowing the lawn in her yoga pants and I must have seen this prick check out her ass at least four times. But wait, before you say it no, I didn't act out about it. I tried to do what you said and "rise above it".

Well done Michael. That there is progress, and a great sign of you controlling this short-tempered rage we have spoken of.

I know right.

So what did you do instead?

I closed the blinds and stuck on a classic movie. Poured myself a drink.

And the kids?

Hell I don't know. Out there doing god knows whatever kids do these days. Meeting up with strangers they met online, smoking pot, playing video-games. That kinda shit. But I digress Doc. That evening I went out for a few drinks with a friend of mine. This swanky little cocktail bar we like in uptown. I took the silver sports coupe and we both got ourselves looking smart. You know, it's good to get out the house some evenings. Good to get out of my own thoughts too. These kinda nights loosen me up ya' know?

Of course, I understand. So... what happened? Anything to tell me about?

There was this hot little pair of girls. Sonia and Monique. We got chatting ya' know, the four of us. They were the typical uptown girls, stilettos, short-skirts, dolled up to the nines. Sexy as hell though.

Did they not care that you were married?

Come on Doc you know I didn't tell them that shit! I left my ring in the glove-box, and my friend, he's single. I mean a man's got to be a man sometimes right? And besides, with that fucking thing going on with Hayden? I never reacted to that.

So this was your way of taking revenge? Sexually rather than violently?

No no Doc you've got it all wrong. I didn't fuck this girl. I just showed her a good time. We kissed a few times but that's nothing is it? My wife will never know and she's probably been out fucking half the neighbourhood. The real fun happened when she asked me how I was getting home. She was going to take a taxi alone because Monique and my friend had been hitting it off all night. I told her "I'll drop you off I came in the coupe" to which she laughed and asked me if I was drunk. "If I can get away with bank robbery I'm sure I can drive home safely" I told her. She thought I was joking.

I hope you got home safely Michael!

I'm here now aren't I? I remember cruising down the freeway under the starlit sky. The moon was so full and clear. Rick James was playing through the radio as I slipped it into 5th gear. Sonia's long beautiful hair blew in the wind like a scene from a movie.

So, you're James Bond now?

Ha! Sorta. Anyway this fucking side of the road hidden in the bushes speed camera must have clocked me getting carried away with myself. All of a sudden, a squad car appeared in my rear-view. This girl nearly shit herself when she saw the blue and red. I ignored the GPS and took the next slip road, pressing harder on the accelerator pedal. "Are we going to be okay?" she asked me. Trembling in the wind. I reassured her everything would be fine before taking a left, a right and then another right swinging the car around the corners. Cars beeped and a few heads turned as I drove us past. I was totally in control. I mean, these situations of high adrenaline come easy to me Doc. The squad car was in pursuit but giving up was never an option.

The girl screamed as I cut in front of this SUV, but I took a few side-roads which led to this multi-story car-park right near the big casino. I switched off the headlights and waited for things to calm down, kissing her passionately in the shadows. Nothing to worry about.

Chapter 17

Mike walked to the pub and picked up another pack of Marlboros on the way. He always smoked more when he was drinking and he knew a proper catch up with Chris meant three or four pints. It was a little breezy on the walk and Mike wished he'd brought a jumper. But he was fine once he got to the Bull's Head. The fire was on, and the atmosphere was cozy rather than crowded. Chris was nowhere to be seen so Mike ordered himself a Smith's and situated himself at one of the small round wooden tables. One thing he liked about the Bull's was that it had no TV's inside. He found TV such a useless distraction these days, and gone were the times he'd go to the pub purely to watch the match and talk football.

He sat there and observed the familiar sights of the pub. The various bottles stood gracefully gathering dust behind the bar. The dartboard and blackboard side by side on the wall. Some chalk scribblings from the last game of Killer. The 'take one leave one' bookshelf with it's copies of *Nicholas Nickelby*, *Catcher in the Rye* and *Fahrenheit 451* amongst heaps of Andy McNab novels and sports autobiographies. He could still smell the after-tones of the roast carvery and vegetable gravy which had been all but cleared away by the teenage kitchen porter.

A pat on his shoulder and a "Long time no see my maan."

"Hey sit down sit down, do you want a pint?"

"If ya don't mind buddy!"

Mike was unsure if that meant he was paying all night. ‘Is his financial situation any better?’ he thought.

"What do you fancy? Shall I get some nuts as well?"

"You've been needin' to grow a pair since 'igh school mate" Chris joked.
"Funny aren't ya?"
"Get us a pint of the 'ouse cider would ya?"
As he was waiting for the pint to be pulled and the peanuts to be put in a bowl, Mike looked back at his old friend. Chris didn't look too great. He wore an old ragged jumper with green and cream stripes, a pair of tatty jeans which appeared to be his only pair, and some trainers which were once white. But more than just his clothes, his face looked wrinkled and worn out. Like a man who's just lost his dog. His physical appearance was an ancient gargoyle, wisely hunched. Cold as stone.

But one should never judge a book by its cover, and Mike knew Chris. Yes he had a problem maintaining a financially stable lifestyle, but he was also wise. Wise like a pensive owl in the night forest.
"So 'ow's the PlayStation Mikey?" Chris smiled.
"You know mate. I've been wondering these last few days who's been doing who the favour!" replied Mike, shuffling back into his chair.
"What dyo' mean man? You sorted me out. And slowly but surely I'm gettin' my shit together"
"Yeah I know, I know that, and it's nothing. I mean I'm hardly Bill Gates myself, but if you need any more just let me know man. However, somehow, someway, that console and that game have been speaking to me. Work's always the same shit, and life at home with Sharon and Toby can get... well... I dunno..."
"I think I get what you're sayin' Mike" Chris said, supping his pint and rubbing the side of his head.
"Everyone needs a little escapism from the real world. Some go the cinema, others sit in front of the TV watchin'

shite reality shows. Some read science fiction novels and superhero comics. It's just preferences innit?"
Mike thought of Kevin at home in his flat. Flicking through a Spiderman graphic novel eating his fishfingers and chips. He chuckled.
"Yeah I guess you're right I never really thought of it like that! But I mean, I'd lost interest in gaming and all that shit. I mean I love the odd game of FIFA round at Tommy or Davo's, but that's a rare thing these days. It's been years since I've actually sat alone and played a game."
"Yeah man yeah, sure, sure" agreed Chris, knocking back the last of his pint.
"And these games have come a long way since *Frogger*," continued Mike. "The graphics have come on so much. They're almost blurring the line between cinema and video-game."
"Defo Mike. Spot on there. People don't always realise the money's in TV Series and blockbuster games these days. I played this one game where you're this guy in this post-apocalyptic world. His daughter gets captured and killed in front of him right at the beginning of the game right"
"Jesus," Mike interrupted, "in the prologue? That sounds brutal"
"Yeah it is. It's a fairly gruesome game to be honest, but the real beauty lies in the character development. The protagonist meets this girl called Ellie, and as the story progresses they form this unique bond. Like, you feel for her..."
Mike nodded his head in understanding before Chris continued, pintless,
"Anyhow this game went on to win over two hundred awards...."
"Sorry Chris do you want another drink mate?"

Chris winced, "If you're sure you don't mind, it's just...."
"Don't worry about it pal. Same?"
“Sure."

When Mike returned with another two pints for the pair of them, Chris continued to inform.
"You do know they use real actors these days too. In games I mean"
"Do you mean voice actors? Like Ray Liotta in *Vice City*?" asked Mike.
"No no I mean, like digitalised motion capture acting performances”. He shifted his chair a little closer.
“Apparently there's this game with Willem Dafoe and Ellen Page, that girl from *Inception*. I haven't played it but I've only heard good things."
The boys were lost in second pint conversation. Talking away whilst the world went by. It was quiet for a Saturday night in the pub.
"I just love the detail and freedom in this latest game" Mike explained, "and the handling of all the vehicles is so finely tuned too. It's as good a driving game as a shooter!"
"Yeah man," said Chris, "it's an all round RPG experience. Listen, ’ave you tried out the first-person mode yet?"
"No. What the fuck?" Mike responded.
"Yeah yeah just press the touchpad and all you can see is the gun in his hand, or the steering wheel when driving of course.”
"Wow I'll have to check that out" Mike said, making a mental note.
"So what's new with you anyway?" It's great to see you again properly Chris"
"Aww cheers man, You too. Nah, nothin’ really. Life ’as just got a little more lonely for me as of late. Our kid moved out a while back after finding this job down south

and, ya know, nothing seems the same since Vic walked out on me"
Chris had lost his childhood sweetheart. As far as Mike could calculate it was a fifteen year relationship.
"Victoria?"
"Yeah I know I know it's fuckin' stupid. It's been a while now but I still think about her."
"That's normal mate. You loved her to pieces back in school, and when you finally got with her..."
"I couldn't believe it" Chris said, finishing the sentence. "I really thought we'd be together forever Mike," he said a little teary-eyed, "I really did."
"I know mate" Mike consoled him, rubbing his shoulder for friendly support, "but life has a funny way of changing for people."
"Tell me about it. To be frank I'm thinkin' about goin' to see a therapist!"
Mike was taken aback,
"Really? Why?"
"'Cause I reckon it'll 'elp with the pain. The feelin' of loss mate. I've been watching a lot of TV Series' with my free time and I could really relate to Tony in *The Sopranos*"
"Haven't seen it mate is it decent?" asked Mike, in some way trying to keep the mood light. He could see Chris slipping into the drink. Emotions bubbling up.
"You need to see it Mike. It's absolutely class. Every episode is like a fuckin' short film."
Chris had those same animated eyes as Rich when he spoke of something he was passionate about. Just with more wrinkles sitting around them.
"Oh yeah I'll have to get onto it. I've heard it's up there as one of the greatest."

Two pints turned into four, and the pair of old friends took regular cigarette breaks in the beer garden out back. The night was on Mike. He really didn't mind either, as he understood that Chris wasn't in the best of places. Mike listened to Chris' speeches about therapy. About this Jennifer Melfi character and stuff about Aristotle and Socrates.

"You always were a good lookin' bastard Mikey" he said as they began to stagger home together down the empty open road. A dog kept barking under the street lights, and the pair spied a fox scurry into the bushes. "I was always a little envious of that."

"Don't be daft you old bastard," said Mike, "you're one of the wisest people I know."

Chapter 18

There was something in a smile. Genuine, false, intended, expected. The smile of a caring mother. A proud teacher. A contented child. Tina had one of those perfect smiles, so full of love and promise. Hardy was sat in his office scrolling through his long list of emails from clients and partners. It was eight-thirty and the first day Mike had arrived to the office early in about five years. Tina was also early as it was her first full week and she, of course, wanted to make a good impression. Mike was just making himself a cup of tea in the cozy confines of the office kitchenette. He watched the teabag diffuse into the boiling water, still half asleep but looking sharp in his new shirt.

"Hey you I don't think we've had a chance to properly meet yet! I'm Tina".

Mike snapped out of his sleepy state and stared straight into her face. Her hazelnut eyes shimmered like that of a baby squirrel.

"Still half asleep?" she asked him, laughing a little as she said it.

"Something like that..." said Mike. It was his go-to phrase when his brain wasn't fully registering.

"Do you fancy a brew?"

"Huh?" replied Tina, "Sorry I don't understand" she blushed. It was then Mike understood. Tina was American.

"You're not British are you?" Mike asked, finally waking up a little bit. He squeezed the teabag against the side of his mug with the first teaspoon within reach.

"As long as you don't think I am Canadian we'll get on just fine..." she said, stopping and staring in seriousness. Mike didn't know what to say. "I'm just joking, yeah I'm American" said Tina, breaking out of her statue and

rubbing Mike on the arm, "and if by 'brew' you mean tea, no I'm aiight but I could go for a green tea if we have it!"
'Did she just touch my bicep?' thought Mike,
"Yeah yeah" he said, fumbling around in the cupboard, "I think we have some at the back here. To be honest nobody in here drinks it."
He found the box somewhere near the back, pulled it out and showed it her,
"Will this do?"
"Perfect" she said without even barely looking at the box.
'God you're amazing!' said the voice in Mike's head, as he was transfixed by her beauty. He grabbed the first mug he could find, rinsed it, and poured the rest of the kettle water onto the green tea bag.
"I'm Mike by the way" he said, as he left her alone by the kitchenette, "nice to meet you but I've got a tonne of work to get started with."
Truth was he just had to get out. He couldn't handle himself properly. Besides the time had just gone five-to, and Kev, Babs and Carol had arrived.
"See ya'll around then" Tina called back to him.

Mike was excited getting back to his chair, and he felt an unrepressed desire to talk to Kev.
"Morning Kev, how was your weekend?"
"Morning Mike. Yeah I had a good weekend, thanks for asking!"
"What did you get up to?"
"Oh nothing too exciting. I had a couple of friends over to watch the remastered original *Star Wars* trilogy" Kev answered, a little awkwardly.
"Oh right" replied Mike, "any good?"
"Yeah it wasn't bad in all fairness. I mean I've seen the originals hundreds of times but never in HD. I didn't much

care for the changing of the ghost scene though in *Return of the Jedi*"
"What's that? I've never really been a big *Star Wars* man myself. In fact, I've never been that big on Sci-Fi."
Kev lifted his eyebrows. He wasn't insulted just a little shocked.
"Basically they replaced the original Anakin - Sebastian Shaw - with Hayden Christensen from the prequels, which, of course, I never really cared for."
They continued to natter away in such fashion, about a number of topics one might consider "geeky". Ian had finally made his grand arrival.
"Morning ladies" he winked at Carol and Barbara,
"Morning Ian" they answered together,
"Morning ladies" he said to Mike and Kev also, swaggering past their desks on his morning office lap. He then head towards Hardy's office wishing Tina a good morning while he was at it. Mike spied Ian laughing away with his boss through the semi-shut blinds of the glass quarters.
"HA HA HA" could be heard by the office.
'I hope that knob isn't laughing about my numbers' thought Mike, who skipped over his four-hundred and twenty-three unread emails. Mike's sales numbers had taken a dive as of late.

He normally popped out for a smoke on his lunch break, and the lift journey down, if alone, was usually a moment of thinking time. Thirteen floors of it. On this particular day he was thinking again about how he'd judged Kevin. He'd played his part in the "Quiet Kev" nickname over the years, and sometimes bad-worded him behind his back. Now he felt bad about it. Like a repentant bully. Kevin was a nice guy. A geek, yes. Or "a nerd" as Ian called him. But what the fuck did that matter Mike thought. Yes

he probably didn't have much luck in the female department but maybe he wasn't even bothered about that? Some people are happy in their own solitude.
'Relationships can cause all sorts of problems' he thought, as the lift sounded its arbitrary ping. He pulled a fag out of his Marlboro box and for some reason put the box into his top shirt pocket.
'Looks cool' he heard a voice say.

A flustered Tina was outside by the smokers step, alone. Looking for something in her handbag.
"Que pasa?" called Mike. Apart from 'Hola' and 'Adios' these were the only Spanish words Mike could remember from his school days. As soon as the words came out of his mouth he felt like a dick. He was trying to be funny but now tried to hold his composure like a stack of Jenga.
Tina smiled that smile.
"Oh it's you Mark" she said surprised, "I'm looking for my fucking lighter, have you got one!?"
The words spat out of her mouth, somewhat sexily.
"It's Mike," he replied, "and no I only lend it to people who know my name."
Tina tilted her head to one side as her curled hair fell gracefully. It was that 'come on give me a break' look.
Mike flicked the underside of his pocket to knock the cigarette box out. His lighter was inside, his straight already in his mouth.
"Smooth" said Tina.
“So, tell me about yourself, what's your story?" asked Mike whilst sparking her up.
Tina took one long deep drag of her Camel cigarette, before tilting her head to the sky and exhaling.
"Thanks," she said, "and oh I didn't realise this was my second interview...."

'Playful' thought Mike.
"No it's not that, it's just hard to get a word in edgeways with Babs and Ian in the office."
"Ha! Tell me about it I hate that jerk already!"
"Wait, what? Ian?" asked Mike in shock, to which Tina nodded her head.
"I'm a pretty good judge of character Mark, I'm great at first impressions" she said, taking in another toke, "my sister too!"
"It's Mike..."
"I know I was just teasing you. Isn't it awful when people get your name wrong?"
Tina oozed confidence and Mike could feel his skin melt inside of it.
"I guess that's right, but yeah. Ian's a prick. I literally hate that guy!"
"Is... that... so?" said Tina.
"It really is. I'm surprised you've managed to hold off his barrage by now"
"I do my best" she replied, which was followed by a short silence. A silence in which Mike got himself another cigarette out.
"Do you want one?" he asked Tina, who had just sat down on the bench and stubbed out her Camel.
"I'm not a chain-smoker Michael" she said boldly, "are you?"
Truth is Mike never had two cigs on his work break, but he had enjoyed his Saturday smoke indulgence with Chris, and he was enjoying time with his co-worker now. He thought about what to say,
"I don't really have any rules with it" he finally came out with.

"Anyway I've been meaning to ask you" said Tina, refusing to react to what Mike had said, "what's the deal with that guy sat next to you? Is he a bit ... I don't know ... geeky? I love geeks!"
Mike couldn't help but laugh.
"I guess you could call him that" replied Mike, "but he's such a nice guy. We have a good laugh together. Yeah. I like Kev."
"I knew it! Kev short for Kevin?" she inquired, her American tones really coming through to Mike now. Tina was different.
"Exactly. I'll have to introduce you. He's not the most talkative of chaps but he's into things like *Star Wars*, *Lord of the Rings, Ghostbusters, Indiana Jones*.... that kinda stuff."
"Perfect! My sister and I are actually massive dorks too, and she's having this sort of, fancy dress party for like, me settling in kind of thing, I dunno. Would you like to come and invite Kev along too?"
Mike literally couldn't believe what he was hearing. He almost choked on his second cigarette, before coughing abruptly, harshly into the clenched fist of his left hand.
"Wait" said Tina. "You're not a geek are you?"
Mike recovered, "I might be".
"Well come on then it'll be cool. And besides, I've not really made any new friends in this neighbourhood.....yet"
"Alright I'll ask him" said Mike, stubbing out his Marlboro and looking at his watch.
"We best go back up" said Tina, "what's your email address? So I can send you over the details."
'Email address? Why not my number or just write down the time and address of the place on a piece of paper' Mike thought.

"Email address? Uhm, yeah, okay, it's Mike, underscore, seventy-six@weboffice.com."
"Great" replied Tina, making a mental note of it, as they head back towards the lift to go back up to work.
'Isn't she going to write it down?'

***

End of Book I

Book II Prologue

The doors closed behind him. His particular carriage empty. A sharp hissing sound signalled the metro engine restarting as the train began to move. He sat down on one of the many grey and blue plastic seats. Observing his closed surrounding. Yellow bars and handrails erected throughout the carriage. Smoking stickers plastered against the glass windows. There was a map stuck to the wall adjacent to the opposite door he entered from. Coloured lines of orange, yellow, green, brown, red, purple scattered and intertwined in all different directions, like an imperfect game of logic. Little white circles with jet black borders dotted themselves all over, but he couldn't figure out the pattern? The carriage kept moving at a slow constant, as he got out of his seat and tried another one. But he couldn't get comfortable. The darkness of the windows signified his feelings. Trapped and alone. He began to wander and pace the cabin which was singular yet adjoined like a pea in its pod. As he stared through the long line of the metro windows, using the artificial lights to help him, the train kept bounding around the turns in the track it followed. Every now and then he caught a glimpse of her. The woman. She was a fair few carriages down from his. Sitting. Reading something in her hands.

***

Chapter 19

Back home in the comfort of his chestnut leather chair, Mike sat and thought. Sharon was out, he had no idea where. He kicked off his work shoes, stretched out his leg muscles and admired his very sweaty socks. It was approaching summer time, and was the kind of day where you change pair midway through the day. A siesta for the feet. Mike hadn't told Kevin about the party yet. He'd decided he was going to wait until the "official" invitation came through. After getting back to his desk from his smoke break, Mike had thought it the right time to sort out his disaster of an inbox. Spam emails, holiday offers, old clients and ticket reservations all discarded to the 'Trash' folder. He hadn't spoken a word with Tina the rest of the working day. But Mike had so many questions inside his thick skull as he sat at home eyes closed.

'How should I convince Kev? How the fuck am I going to get a fancy dress outfit? What shall I go as? Where is the place? When is the party? Why did she ask for my email? Why didn't she just write the address in my phone? Why was she avoiding my questions? What should I tell Sharon?'

He got up and poured himself a glass of water. Toby was nowhere to be seen as Mike opened up the fridge-freezer and grabbed himself a Hawaiian pizza. He stuck it in the oven on 200 degrees, and made his mind up to avoid it all and have a go on his game. Take his mind off things.

Driving on the game was so much more fun than driving in real life. Firstly, Mike could choose to steal any vehicle he wanted. Secondly he could avoid all the rules of the road. Thirdly the radio adverts were fewer and far more satirical, and finally, Mike could unload his pistol on any passerby that pissed him off. A simple drive-by on a local gang of hoodlums could result in a three star police chase through the city streets and past the west coast beach. It didn't matter how many times he crashed his vehicle into something, or how many vehicles he overturned and exploded. This was his playground. A playground for adults loaded with violence, speed and shooting. On this particular session, Mike remembered the first-person mode Chris had told him of. He held down the touch-pad as instructed, and all of a sudden his world transformed. He was the eyes. He pulled out his pistol for protection and started running, breathing. He was in the Vinewood district, apparent from the sheer amount of flashy cars and stuck-up pricks that were around him. He was just crossing over the road by one of the large movie theaters, when a white limousine bumped into him, knocking him over in the middle of a busy road.

"You fucking little…" he said, before dragging the chauffeur out of the drivers door, head first. Mike looked down at the driver, waiting for him to get up, like a boxer on a 7 count. Once he got up off the road, Mike swung his right fist and lamped the driver on the side of his face. A perfect punch. Then he swung his left, and then his right again, until the chauffeur was unconscious on the road, his face a midnight purple. Mike laughed to himself,

"Ha that'll teach you, you little fucker!"

However the scene had only just begun. As Mike moved his protagonist off the road to the sidewalk, he looked around to see a pile up of vehicles behind the limo and the battered driver. A large, beefed-up man with a bald head got out of the back of the limo and shouted something inaudible. He flossed three big bulky chains, was wearing a knuckle-duster and he looked extremely angry. Mike

readied his fists, and kept his vision locked on the muscle man. Anticipating his first move. A crowd was beginning to gather, ready to view the fight like a group of excited school kids. The meat head swung his fist as a street brawler would. Mike reacted, dipping his left shoulder and ducking his head, so that he just glimpsed the shiny silver of the steel duster smooth past his face. His opponent's chest was open, so Mike unleashed a barrage of strong punches which forced the VIP to curl over and fall to the floor. Fully winded.
Mike laughed again.
"Ha, didn't even need any weapons"
He began kicking the meat head. Kicking his face repeatedly as blood gushed out of his nose and onto the concrete. It was a graphic scene to be witnessed from bare eyes. Unfortunately, another set of eyes had witnessed the brutality. A police officer who had been passing the scene on his motorcycle had pulled up onto the sidewalk and had already begun to radio back to the station. Sirens could be heard in the distance as panic spread like wildfire. It was Mike's time to escape. He ran, left right left right down the side of the cinema which led to a passageway, pushing a few pedestrians out of the way as he went. No time to look back. But he could hear the police bike engine following him. One passage led to another with a low-level gate half way along it. Mike sprinted towards the gate and shuffled over it like some street free-runner. Immediately over, he turned, and saw the motorcyclist cop facing him. He turned his sirens on which blinded the darkness of the backstreets with ear piercing blue and red flashes. Things were starting to get out of hand so Mike aimed his .45 at the officer and pulled the trigger four times. Bullet one missed completely, bullet two hit the target's helmet and ricocheted off. Bullet

three hit the officer in the leg and four direct in the chest. Mike turned and moved in the direction he was heading. The passageway came out onto a suburban residential road as a storm gathered overhead. A pair of officers appeared to his left so he shot at them too, unloading the rest of his clip. His aim was near perfect this time as both officers went down. The sound of helicopter blades could be heard, just as Mike spied a dirt bike pulled up on someone's drive.
"That's mine" he said, as he jumped on and kick-started the engine. The bike was easy to handle as Mike weaved in and out of traffic, heading north towards the mountains. He had to get out of the city. The bike went off-road, jumping over hills and catching air. The chopper had appeared in front of him and a sniper had taken position leaning out of the left shutter. Mike saw the red laser taking aim at him and he pulled harder on the accelerator handle. A squad car was now in pursuit, rolling over the hills, and four men had begun sliding down a rope dropping down from the right side of the helicopter. There was a barn in the distance which Mike could take shelter at. But a stray bullet caught his front tyre. It forced the protagonist to jump off the bike and continue on foot. He was breathing heavily now. Sprinting as fast as he could.
"What the?" he heard a voice say, and then nothing. A black mirror.

Sharon had arrived home to find her husband completely transfixed on Chris' PlayStation. Annoyed at his obliviousness and the smell of burning pizza, she had turned the TV off to prove a point.
"MIKE! I thought we spoke about, A) answering my messages and, B) keeping an eye on things in the oven!"
"Shit, I'm sorry" he said, all the time wondering what was happening in the police chase.

"I've been trying to get in touch with you for the past forty-five minutes " she said, frustratedly, whilst turning off the oven.
"Sharon I've said I'm sorry what more do you want!?" Mike answered, raising his tone and turning the TV back on.
"Don't raise that voice at me Mike. Don't you dare!" said Sharon.
The screen read: WASTED as Mike saw himself spread murdered on the field. Cops had surrounded him and aimed their pistols at his corpse.
Then he re-spawned outside the hospital.

Chapter 20

The married couple had an argument before going to bed. Stuff about responsibility, finances and lack of quality time spent. Like a lot of their arguments it carried through to the next morning, which they both spent in silence. Mike made breakfast for himself, and ignored the ever-whimpering Toby who was lay down, bored as always. As he drove to work, he popped a CD on in the car to try and block out once more, those questions which lay dozing on his brain.

'I wonder if she's sent that email yet' he thought as the traffic light showed red. Mike tapped his feet against the pedals, timely to the beat. The sun had risen and was heating up the fresh morning air.

As he shifted from 1st to 2nd gear, and span his sedan around the corner, he saw his nephew waiting at the bus stop, looking at his watch. Mike pulled up right next to him,

"Where you goin' Rich? What you doin'?"

Rich was just as surprised to see his Uncle.

"Waiting for the bus home, are you on your way to work Uncle Mike?"

Mike looked at his watch. It read quarter-to-nine.

"Yeah I am yeah but don't worry I'll give you a lift. Jump in!"

"No, no, honestly I wouldn't want to make you late!"

"Just shut up and get in" Mike said.

Truth is Mike was probably going to be a little late but he really didn't mind. Yes it clashed against his 'early bird catches the worm' plan but Mike was proud of being a good Uncle. Besides he had no idea what Rich was doing at this time of the day.

"What you doin' here anyway?" Mike asked again.
Rich looked rather down, his head lower than usual.
"Mum asked me to spy on Dad"
It was a statement so cold and hollow, like a bloodless heart.
"What?" said Mike, "Why?"
"She thinks he has a gambling problem. And, his timetable seems to have been all out of sorts. They haven't been to the gym together in like, two weeks."
"I haven't been to the gym in like, fifteen years" Mike replied, desperate to try and lighten the poor kid's mood.
Rich managed a brief laugh, but he was trapped in his mood. An emotionally wounded animal.
"So what have you discovered?" Mike asked his nephew, knowing it was impossible to avoid the subject.
"Well, I think she's right. I saw him leave the bookies this morning. About twenty-five minutes ago. Must have been an overnight "lock-in" as he calls them."
"That's poker for you son" replied Mike, who immediately felt a little awkward. Mike never normally called Rich "son". It was a habit he must have picked up from his Grandad, who always used to say it to him.
"Yeah" replied Rich, "and the rest of it. Blackjack, roulette, the football, the horses, the fucking greyhounds."
"I know what you mean" said Mike, heading towards his nephew's road.
"Dad's changed" said Richie.
"Try not to overthink it too much Rich. Just tell your mother what you saw and leave it at that. I know you're only seventeen, but you're a smart kid. Smart enough to know marriage can be a complicated thing."
"I know" responded his nephew, before asking his Uncle to drop him at the end of the road.

"Call me if you need me" Mike shouted out the window, as Rich walked off towards his house.

He was ten minutes late for work, and thus, he knew he would be office gossip. When the lift doors opened on floor thirteen, everyone was in their proper places, behind keyboards tapping away. Everyone stared at him, like he was the latest media scandal.

"I think Hardy wants a word with you!" blurted out Babs, with a cheeky eye-roll to complement it.

"I gathered" replied Mike, who wandered over to the glass office.

As he approached the door, Ian muttered something about his office brew mug but before Mike could even register what he was saying, he shut him off,

"Oh fuck off not now."

It was loud enough for Tina to hear and she watched Ian's face for it's reaction. Red.

"Michael Michael Michael" said Mr Hardy, shaking his head and tutting.

"Or Mike" suggested Mike.

"Or whatever I want your name to be" said his boss, putting his foot down.

"You listen to me and listen good" said Hardy, lowering the blinds.

"I pride myself on running a good office sector. I pride my team on strong work ethic. No no no" Hardy continued, clicking his pen frantically, "you may think that you're in here because you were ten minutes late today, but that's simply not the case. Of course punctuality is one of my," he stroked his skinny tie, "pet peeves, shall we say? But what's more is ..... your sales records stink."

Mike knew this to be true, so he just kept his mouth shut and listened. Hardy was pissed.

"I mean I know you're one of the lesser earners in this office, and have been for quite some years now." Hardy nodded a patronising grin. "But this year you've hit a new low."
"I understand" Mike replied, with an ever-so-slight hint of teenage cockiness in his tone.
"And what's more" continued Hardy, "we've been blessed with the lovely Tina, who has a great track record in sales Mike, and who is, quite frankly, propping you up right now. Balancing out the averages kind of thing."
'Tina is beautiful' thought Mike.
Hardy's rant was coming to and end.
"Now I expect you've got some bullshit sob-story to tell me about why you couldn't get to work on time this fine Tuesday morning but frankly I don't want to hear it."
Mike nodded, and thought of Rich.
"Now get to your desk and start upping the ante Mike, because the ice beneath your feet is thinning!"

Mike exited Hardy's office, blanked Ian and Tina to his right, smiled falsely to Babs and Carol and seated himself in his place.
"Morning Kev" he said, whilst logging into the server using his password, which happened to be his wife's name backwards.
"Morning Mike, hope it wasn't too bad"
"Nothing to worry about" Mike replied, heading straight to his emails.
There it was. The email from Tina. It read:

Mark,

This is your "official" invitation to the best and geekiest fancy dress party in the history of humanity. You can bring a plus one and you know who I want you to invite. The address is 34 Highgate Avenue. Friday at 9pm. Don't be late ;)

Tina

p.s. Let's continue to keep this our secret. Don't want the whole office knowing....

Nightmares

What would you like to talk about today Michael?

How about the fact that deep down I hate my life? Is that a good subject Doc?

That depends. You are paying to come to these sessions Michael.

Yeah I know, and sometimes I think it's one big waste of fucking money. I mean, couldn't I just speak to the local drunk at the park if I wanted to get all philosophical?

You could but you can also talk to a trained professional. What do you want to get off your chest?

I'm a bad person Doc. I ain't a good role model.

How so?

Because I'm outta control sometimes. I've spent time in prison, I have more money than sense, and I think I have an anger problem.

You've experienced a lot of excitement doing what you do Michael. Of course I think your self-loathing is born out of a life of falsehood, but you really shouldn't be so hard on yourself. Positivity can be fundamental to achieving success here.

...........I know. I mean sure, my life is, on paper, kinda luxurious. But I'm having nightmares Doc. People don't seem to know the real me. I feel like I've lived and died a hundred times. Just the other day I saw this fruit vendor at the side of this dusty desert road. 'Peaches, Apples, Bananas' his sign read. Cars were zipping past, not one of them pulling over. So I did. I approached him and aimed my gun at his fucking head. But before I knew it he started running and moved straight past me into the road which had multiple lanes. I was pissed by this point. My blood started boiling. So I ran after him and fired stray bullets in his direction. I was trying to take him down. I kept missing though, so instinctively I started chasing him. Not looking where I was going at all.

And then.....

And then a huge fucking truck carrying a boat on its back trailer, hit me at some serious speed. I heard my bones crunch as it sent me into the road. The last thing I can remember is a faded buzz of the fruit seller running off into the distance.

I'm not too sure what you want me to say Michael. Rage must be calmed by reaching inner peace. I mean, are you looking for a Freudian interpretation of this event?

I don't want that shit Doc. I just wanna get out......

Chapter 21

"Kevin" whispered Mike.
"Ttsssst, hey Kevin?"
Kevin was a little hard of hearing, and he was wearing his headset and spectacles like a man on a mission. Cracking codes. Unlike Mike, Kevin took his job seriously, probably because he was quite good at it.
"Kev!" Mike whispered again. Not wanting to draw any more attention to himself. He looked around the office and fortunately, everyone was in work mode.
"Kev...are you....", he tapped him,
"Yes Mike I'm sorry I was just playing something"
"Yeah, I gathered", said Mike, "what is it?"
"Oh nothing just some new MMO I wanted to check out"
"Oh yeah....well check this out for size" said Mike, beckoning Kevin to come and have a look at his screen.
"Is this from Ti-"
"Sssshhhhh, Kev, Kev, it's a secret alright, keep it down!"
Kevin continued reading through the email,
"Geekiest? .... Plus one? .... Winky face", he muttered, "well?" he asked, looking at Mike.
"Well what?"
"Well how did all this come about and why are you showing it to me?" Kevin asked, rearranging and cleaning his glasses.

Hardy came out of his glass office and began surveying his workers. Who was slaving away and who was slacking off? Kevin wheeled himself and his leather chair back behind his computer. He was a plump fellow but Hardy didn't notice him. To Babs' pleasant surprise he had gone over to have a chat with her and Carol.

"I showed *you* Kevin" Mike explained through a tightened jaw, "because you're the plus one she wants me to invite. I mean," he stumbled, "I want you to be my plus one too!"
Kevin was taken aback.
"Have you two been speaking about me? Is this some kind of joke Mike?"
Both of them pretended to be hard at work when Hardy lifted his head and walked towards them.
"Working hard chaps?" he said with his best smile.
"Sure am"
"Yep", they replied.
"Good" said Hardy before turning and walking away.

Mike suggested lunching together that day. So when the break came the two of them walked past the usual cafe, to this new Americanised diner that had recently opened a few streets down. They ordered their burgers and spicy french fries and then Mike gave a more thorough explanation. He told Kev what had happened over that cigarette break and that Tina's sister was hosting the party.
"She wants to get to know us Kev!"
"Why?" he answered,
"She loves geek apparently! She's a geek herself!"
Kevin was confused, "But you're not a geek and, and, Tina doesn't look like one either let's be honest!"
"Who the fuck cares Kev!? said Mike, rather loudly, just as the waitress brought over the food.
"Me and you have been invited to sexy Tina's secret party and there is no invite for anyone else on floor thirteen!"
Kevin was taking it all in as he squirted ketchup and mustard on the underside of his bun, and spread it all together with his knife.
"Why?"

"Well," said Mike taking the first chomp of his bacon double cheese, "because she thinks Ian's a dick and I don't think she's interested in joining the loose-women clan."

Kevin laughed, "When is it again?"

Teeth ground and chewed and cut through the meat as the saliva glands spat out more liquid. The hot cheese oozed between their incisors and canines.

"Friday, what do you think?" asked Mike excitedly, impatiently.

"I'm not sure" said Kevin, "and I've got plans."

Mike could tell Kev was lying. He was sliding into the comfort of his snail shell.

"Bollocks, you're coming!" Mike instructed, "I need you there. I scratch your back you scratch mine. Come on, it's exciting and you know it! No doubt her sister is just as cool as she is, and there'll be more geeks than a sci-fi convention."

Kevin looked at Mike like he'd just misquoted a classic *Star Wars* line.

"Fine I'll come."

Tuesday carried on in its typical drawn-out fashion. The weekend was far away and now that Hardy was onto Mike, he actually had to start doing some work. Phone-calls, emails, facts, figures; Mike was growing tired of this job. Too many years, too little variety.

"What should I go as?" he asked Kevin, as he procrastinated from his office work.

"No idea Mike, but you better get thinking. It's three days from now."

"True" Mike replied,

"And", continued Kevin, "if you don't get a costume I'm not going at all"

"Fair enough, don't worry" said Mike, "I'll think of something."
"Is this even a secret from your wife?" asked Kevin, scratching the side of his head.
"Yes" said Mike, staring seriously into Kevin's eyes, “it is.”

Chapter 22

Mike's mind was so transfixed on Friday night, that the next couple of work days rolled into one. He was hooked on anticipation, yet he didn't want to give off the overly-excited impression. Not to Kevin, not to Tina, not to Sharon. In the office he kept himself to himself. His work output had increased, but he was also surfing the web, losing himself in digital tangents. He'd read online somewhere that unpredictability was exciting, and helped to crank up attraction. Thus, he acted incredibly nonchalant about Tina's invitation.

"Did you tell Kevin?" Tina had asked him on the Wednesday.

"What are you coming as?" she asked him on the Thursday.

"We're not sure what our plans our yet" he'd replied, in an attempt to build up suspense.

Truth was, Mike had no fucking idea what to go as. He wasn't much into fantasy stuff, he'd never been into sci-fi, and even Harry Potter he had found a bit dull. Heath Ledger's 'Joker' had been done to death and a superhero costume was, well, a little predictable. To make things worse he couldn't browse or think out-loud at home. Sharon couldn't know about any of it and Toby put Mike on edge with his 'all-knowing' stares. Mike ignored Toby and glued himself to his worn leather chair. It was Thursday evening and his laptop was open and on his lap, the clogged fan heating up his legs and singeing his skin through his trousers. Sharon kept talking at him, but Mike was a phantom. There but not really. His web browser was filled with various pages and forums about fancy-dress outfits. Of course, he hadn't told Sharon, who kept wandering past and taking the occasional glance at the screen. As a cover up,

Mike had loaded up his old bookies account, and was in the process of arranging a well-calculated accumulator.

"What are your plans for the weekend honey?" asked Sharon. The inevitable question. Mike's phone pinged, it was Kevin.

"Eerrm..." Mike responded, weighing up his lie, "I'm actually meeting up with a few of the old lads. Bit of a football weekend."

"Football! Really? I thought those days were behind you Mike!"

'You're so fucking annoyingly inquisitive' Mike thought, avoiding a verbal response, instead opting to read Kev's message:

Costume sorted. Nervous about tomorrow but also excited. R U ready? Kev.

Mike's fingers slipped and slid all over the screen:

Don't worry everything will be fine. C U 2morrow

"I'm making a pasta bake love" said Sharon, as she lurked behind his shoulders again.

"Perfect" said her husband, adding an eighth game to his accumulator, increasing the odds and the payout.

They sat opposite each other at dinner, as Sharon divided the pasta bake into six square pieces inside the Pyrex dish.

"Sorry hun, I burnt the cheese a little"

"No worries Shaz" replied Mike, sliding the spatula underneath a piece, carefully lifting. Toby grumbled, but refused to eat his meaty chunks.

"What's with that dog?" exclaimed Mike. Sharon let out a sigh.

"I think he's poorly Mike. Poor pooch hasn't been his usual self recently"

"You're telling me!"

"That makes Toby *and* Tony" said Sharon, rolling her eyes and sucking her fork.
Mike watched Toby tilt his head to one side, his black eyes vacant, his dripping muzzle shivering gently, his tail still and limp. Sharon spoke and spoke about what her sister had been telling her. Tony's gambling problem had been getting worse, leaving his wife unsatisfied, their bank accounts depleted and their son disengaged.
"He's a prick. Plain and simple." Mike said, scoffing his meal, "He's got a great wife, and that kid deserves better!"
Sharon's brain rattled inside her skull. She agreed with her husband about Tony, but disagreed with his language. Mike wasn't one to normally swear. Sharon fiddled with her food, and tapped her foot unknowingly under the kitchen table. To her, the comment about her sister was unnecessary, and she thought,
'Why the fuck is he so warm towards Richie, but so cold on the idea of us having a child?'

Mike thought about what Michael would do. Michael didn't worry about such peculiarities.
'Fuck it' he thought, during the rest of dinner's silence. 'I'm overthinking the fancy-dress, and I need to release some stress.'
"Don't worry about the dishes Shaz" he said, standing and grabbing her hand. Mike took charge and began to lead her upstairs. Sharon felt confused. He jogged up the stairs, dragging her along with him. Kicking open the bedroom door he tossed her onto the bed.
"I'm going to fuck you now baby" he half-whispered, hitching up her skirt and pulling her knickers to one side.
"Wh-where has all this come from Mike?" asked Sharon, trying her hardest to lose herself in the moment. Mike never answered the question. He unzipped his fly, pulled it

out and drilled his wife from behind. Thrusting, thinking about other things.

Chapter 23

It was Friday morning. Mike woke alone. He could hear his wife downstairs pottering about and could also hear a couple of birds tweeting by the window. His phone light was flashing blue, indicating unread emails rather than standard texts. For some reason his phone was now linked up to his email account, though this was not of his own doing. 'Must have updated automatically' he thought, heading into his inbox. Just the usual junk.

Downstairs Sharon was quiet. Unusually so.

"You okay?" Mike asked, popping a tea bag into his mug.

"Yeah fine" replied Sharon.

Mike felt like he should dig a little, much to her frustration. He asked more questions from softening angles, but to very little avail. Sharon had made a point not to reveal any doubts or insecurities, which played on Mike's paranoia.

Shutting it all out of his mind, he left the house and jumped into his car. The sun was out so he banged on his shades and rolled the window down a little to let in some morning air. Then he set off to the petrol station to pick up some fags. It was the same blonde with the baby blue eyes that served him.

"Marlboros" he said with a smile, lowering his sunglasses.

The girl returned with his box of cigarettes, and silently hit the keys on the till.

"Six-ninety" she smiled cutely, just as Mike slipped his wallet out of his pocket and remembered he had no cash.

"Any petrol today?" she asked, if only to kill the silence.

"Can I pay on card?" he asked in return, sliding it out and offering it to her.

"Yep, of course you can" she said nicely, as her cold trembling fingertips gently brushed his finger upon collection.

On top of forgetting to withdraw cash, Mike couldn't find his lighter, and he had forgotten to charge his phone overnight.

'She might message' he thought, before remembering not to worry and keep in line with a collected persona. Mike had decided during the night's tossing and turning that he was going to play things safe in relation to the fancy-dress outfit. He was suiting up, and that was that. If anyone asked who he was he would tell them "James Bond" or "Bruce Wayne" or any other suave sophisticated male with secrets. So he dropped off his crumpled trousers, shirt and dinner jacket (which had been living in his boot) at the dry-cleaners, and then he arrived to work.

Kevin was nowhere to be seen at the office. Mike thought he was probably late until nine rolled into half-past, half-past rolled into ten, and ten rolled on into midday.

'I wonder where he is?' he thought. 'He better not be fucking ill'. 'I can't go on my own tonight'. 'He's letting me down here'.

For all his supposed calmness, Mike's brain had been busy of late. Thoughts peppering like machine-gun shells.

'Life was so much easier as a child, when video games meant everything and the worst thing about real life was a sheet of Maths and English homework on a Friday.'

The office was quiet and functioning. Hardy wasn't in either, which meant it was just Mike, Babs, Carol, Tina and Ian, the latter of whom had been left in charge by Hardy. Luckily that meant Ian was up to his eyeballs in admin, but because he was sat next to Tina, Mike couldn't really approach her and enquire about the night's proceedings. He

hoped that Ian still didn't know about it and Tina hadn't invited him out of pity at the last moment. Life outside the office in a social environment with that dickhead was simply unthinkable.
Trying to get his head down to the day's tasks was difficult. The aching walls stared at him. The peeling wallpaper whispered. Panicking somewhat, Mike wrote an email to Kev, now that his mobile was defunct.
"Where are you? What's going on? Don't let me down buddy" he punched into the keys. It was one of those frantic emails you didn't check over before slamming the send button.

Helplessly, Mike kept finding his vision magnetised to Tina. She couldn't see him looking at the shape of her neck, or the gold zipper that fastened her pencil skirt. Tina was so elegant. A modern professional who embodied style and conviction. It occurred to Mike that the night ahead he would see her out of her work attire, in an unprofessional environment. He just had to make sure that Kevin was still game.

Postcards

Welcome to today's session Michael. How are you feeling today? A little...better than last time?

Yeah thanks for asking Doc. I'm feeling pretty good today. My mother always told me you gotta take the highs with the lows.

Your mother?

Seriously, not now. I don't want to talk about her right now. I'm not in the mood for your bullshit Oedipus complex thanks.

I understand....so....are you in the mood to tell me why you're "feeling pretty good today"?

Yeah, that's more like it! Well, where should I start? Oh right yeah. So I was out back by the pool smoking a cigar and thinking about the glory days. When all of a sudden the other half shouted me. Basically I got this pen-pal who lives up in the middle of nowhere. He sends me postcards now and then and I always enjoy them. I find there's something therapeutic about writing. Unlike my son for example. All he enjoys is playing dumb video games where all he does is shoot shit. Nah, I guess I'm old fashioned or something.

I like your style Michael. I always find writing to be a cathartic experience. Reading's great for the brain also. Do you read much?

Not really. You know me I prefer a classic movie.

Right...

Anyway... this pen-pal, well, friend of mine - let's call him Tommy - we used to hang out a lot in our younger days. Goofin' around, drinkin', smokin', talkin' about girls and that sorta stuff. And I gots to thinkin'....life changes. I mean, of course it does that's fuckin' obvious, but. There's stages, you know?

Well...yeah....but go on.

I mean people always say, "Life begins at Forty" and shit. But does it? I mean this postcard I received. It was cool to hear from him - Tommy - but at the same time the content was pretty dull. Tommy's now late forties just like me. He's married with kids just like me.

He sounds settled.

Exactly! Safe and sound. But back then, in our twenties, we were outta control, I mean Doc, every other night meant whiskey and narcotics. We'd stay in listening to old records, or we'd head out into the nightlife with a billion choices at our disposal.

This was back before the heist days, right?

Right. Back before I had a care in the world. Back before responsibilities and electricity bills and shit.

I mean time shifts, and even though life is this open grandeur, this unraveling ball of string, it's like no matter how hard one tries, you'll inevitably reach this plateau. Back then in our late teenage years, we were fuckin' beautiful girls, drinkin' like fish and smokin' like chimneys - all guilt free.
I remember this one time we got invited to this frat party thing. Tommy knew one of the girls who was the daughter of a family friend or somethin'. Now let me tell you Doc this place was wild. I mean, wild. The girls too. Everyone was drinkin' vodka shots, passin' joints and laughin' all night long. I know you always tell me I like to reminisce but, it's hard not too!

Michael it's completely natural to remember joyous times of youth. There's no harm in looking back once in a while.

But can we ever go back? Can't we drop real life and go back to that free-spirited place? That feeling of invulnerability? I mean we're animals aren't we? Hot blooded mammals trapped in the digital age.

And you feel? Trapped? Trapped inside some sort of digital cage?

Well, sorta! Don't you? I mean those sorta nights back then, you were free. A young man just settin' out on your grand exploration. Except the treasure back then was unknown. The truth ain't all it's cracked up to be. Back in those bachelor days we were popping strange pills and snortin' cocaine off of hot chicks' nipples. Now I'm talking to my therapist weekly, arguing with my gold-digger wife and completely failing to inspire my teenage son and daughter.

Let me tell you somethin' Doc. Adulthood comes with a whole lotta consequences. And lord knows I've been dealt my fair share of those.

This is all very interesting Michael. But I'm afraid that's all we've got time for today.

Chapter 24

The time was eight thirty and Mike was making his way down Highgate Avenue, which, for an 'avenue', was fairly long. Crushing clouds stared down from their thick faces, as they cried gently on the hard concrete. The wet air smelt fresh though, despite the puddles grim reflections from the bouncing lights of the lampposts. Mike was alone, and had been since he'd finished work. After picking up his suit he'd driven his car to an NCP and got changed awkwardly in the back seat.

Mike had resigned to the fact that Kevin was sick and wouldn't be coming, despite sending him numerous text messages after managing to find a spare charger at work and charging his phone a little. Now in the wet late evening, droplets appeared on his touch screen, revealing that shiny rainbow effect.

"Are U com-" he began to type, head down striding towards his destination. But the touch keyboard wasn't functioning in the rain. His frustration levels were rising, as his trousers dampened and his phone disappointed him.

"Fucking Kevin" Mike said aloud, kicking a bunch of soggy leaves. "Where the fuck is he? He's proper let me down."

Just as he was complaining, he spotted a newsagents on one of the corners. He was agitated and outside number 56 so there wasn't far to go. Mike also had no booze. The only thing he did have was his grandfathers old hip-flask, which had been gathering dust inside the glove-box of his car. He'd grabbed it before leaving the NCP, because upon shaking it, he'd realised a fermented concoction of old scotches had infused. As Mike stared at the huntsman and

stag which were etched onto the flask, he could hear the soft demanding words of his dear Grandfather:
"Never rinse it out son. To do that is pure sacrilege."
Thus, Mike never put water into the flask. He simply topped it up with new whiskies and bourbons.

The bell pinged as he opened the corner shop door and scraped his soles on the bristly mat. A shriveled woman pottered around behind the counter, moving items ever so slightly as to give the illusion of perfect order.
"What would you like love?" she asked, revealing smoke-stained yellow teeth and a ripple of sunken wrinkles that curled the corner of her lips. Mike surveyed the brown and clear glass bottles behind the counter and inquired about the bourbons.
"Rich Gentleman. One litre. S'all we've got I'm afraid"
"No smaller bottles?" asked Mike, to which the shriveled lady shook her head.
"Then that'll do then" said Mike, wondering how on earth he was going to get through it all. He handed the woman a couple of crumpled notes, then exited the shop with his bottle.

The rain was still bouncing which added to the stress of transferring the Rich Gentleman from the bottle to the flask. This wasn't how Mike had imagined the night would start. It wasn't smooth. It wasn't slick. So he tried his utmost to catch the light from a lamp post so that he could pour the liquid carefully, but it gurgled out of the bottle, spilling all over his hand that was holding the flask.
"Fuck!" he exclaimed, "now I need some fucking tissues...."
"AND MY AXE!"

Mike looked up. It was Kevin, dressed like an old dwarven warrior. He wore a fake platted beard and plenty of brown leather. In his right hand he held a short battleaxe.
"Okay, who the fuck have you come as?" asked Mike, shaking his hand dry from the spillage. "Come here buddy" he followed up with, delighted to see his partner in crime.
"Don't you know who I am?" asked Kevin, opening his arms to a warm embrace, "I'm Gimli...."
There was a moment of dampened silence.
"......from *Lord of the Rings*!"
"Ohh" replied Mike, "I told you I've never been much into fantasy or sci-fi shit."
Kevin reacted in his usual bewildered manner.
"I can see that Mike" he said, looking him up and down, "what have you come as?"
Mike placed the flask and the bourbon down on the wet pavement, dusted himself off and straightened his tie.
"I'm Bruce Wayne, Gotham's favourite millionaire philanthropist"
"Ahh I see" said Kevin, a little unimpressed, "so you don't like *fantasy* but you like men who dress up in bat costumes?"
"Something like that…Anyway, where the fuck have you been Kev? I've been trying to get hold of you. I thought you'd left me high and dry."
"Give me some of that you've got there and I'll explain" said Kevin, "besides, haven't we got a party to get to?"

In that moment the clouds softened. The rain turned to a lighter drizzle as the two middle aged men continued down the avenue. Kevin explained his absence was due to a virus that had corrupted his computer files.
"I wasn't going to come" he explained, "but losing most of my files and stressing out and stuff. It got me thinking I

need to do something different, something drastic, and well...", Kevin swung his battle-axe around, "...look at me now!"
The atmosphere became jovial between them, as they discussed the oddities of work and glugged from the bottle of Rich Gentleman. Their bodies loosened as the brown liquor seeped into their kidneys. They had arrived. Number 34.

Chapter 25

A sharply dressed man in his early thirties answered the door. He wore a suit with a loose white shirt underneath. His hair was slicked back and the instrument which had aided him to do so, rested in the breast pocket of his suit jacket. Dark wayfarer sunglasses covered his eyes, but he was charismatic and open considering he had never met Bruce or Gimli before.
"Welcome to the party guys" he exclaimed extending his arm for a handshake,
"I'm Jack nice to meet y'all, welcome to our flat!"
"Nice to meet you" said Kevin.
"Yeah nice to meet you" said Mike, "we're erm, friends of Tina."
They stepped through the front door into the flat.
"Ohh yeah you're the guys from work right? Tina's told me all about it. I'm Jack her cousin. Welcome to my pad make yourselves comfortable!"
Jack swaggered through the living room with the guests in tow. He was in a jubilant mood and was evidently proud of his abode. Movie stills scattered the walls and there were an array of different lamps and speakers.
"Nice place" stated Mike, 'where's Tina?' he thought.
Jack picked up on it as he began to introduce Mike and Kevin to the other more punctual guests.
"Tina and Dawn aren't here at the moment, I think they're still preparing a few things but let me introduce you to some people, this is Rose, this is Rachel and this is Clara."
'Where the fuck am I?' thought Mike, intrigued by their unique names, blue painted bodies and strange haircuts.
"Hi, I'm.....well I'm Kevin" he choked a little, "but tonight I'm a dwarven warrior", he stuttered nervously. The girls,

dressed as *Avatars* giggled upon being greeted. Mike simply shook their hands.

"Let me take you through here...." Jack looked at Mike, trying to remember if he had given his name.

"Mike"

"That's the one sorry buddy"

Jack beckoned Mike to follow him, which he did, whilst Kevin seated himself on the black leather sofa near to the *Avatar* girls.

"This is a pretty modern place innit" said Mike, conscious that he kept mentioning the place.

"D'ya like it?" asked Jack, his American tones coming through, "wait until you see this room. Fancy a drink?"

A type of mellow dance music came through the wall mounted speakers as Jack led Mike into another room.

"This" said Jack, extending his arms like an eagles wings, "is what I like to call the man cave…"

"Fuck, me!" was the only response Mike could muster. The room was a sort of paradise. There was a billiard table in the centre, a private corner bar with an ice-cold beer tap, bottles on shelves behind, Tarantino, Kubrick and Scorsese pictures hung on the walls, and a few large comfortable seats were at the sides. Mike took a seat on one of the three black leather bar stools whilst Jack prepared three glasses with ice.

"What are you boys drinkin tonight?" asked Jack, even though Mike was the only other person in the man cave.

Due to the fact that Jack was so slick, Mike felt the need to slip into character. He pulled out his hip-flask from his inside pocket.

"Ahh you're a whiskey man, I like it" said Jack, "bourbon or scotch?"

"Bourbon" answered Mike as Jack spun around and ran his index finger along a line of bottle necks.
"This will do us" Jack said, selecting the bottle, unscrewing the cap and pouring the brown liquid over the crackling ice. As he did so, Mike felt a slight of embarrassment at his bottle of Rich Gentleman, which fortunately, Kevin had offered to keep in his satchel.
"Is there a place to smoke around here?" asked Mike, remembering he had a couple of Marlboros left.
"Sure thing Mike you can smoke one right here. Or out back if you prefer, the door is just through the kitchen."
"Right here will do if you don't mind" replied Mike, still feeling a little apprehensive. "Do you want one?" he offered Jack, opening the box lid.
"Sure, thanks. Hey, do you and your friend like billiards, pool, snooker or whatever y'all call it?"

Kevin was still with the *Avatar* girls when Mike went back into the living room. He had settled into the gentle ambience of the room, evident from the Rich Gentleman bottle which he was glugging from upon seeing Mike.
"Mike, this is Aidan" yelled Kevin, introducing Mike to a tall, thin man dressed up as Captain Jack Sparrow.
"Nice to meet you" said Mike, shaking Captain Jack's hand before coaxing Gimli to stand and follow him. There was still no sign of the sisters, which again gave Mike that feeling that things weren't quite going as imagined.
"Kev, wait till you see this room. Jack's got us covered tonight."
"Why, what's happening?" replied a slightly intoxicated Kevin.
"Oh nothing he's just got his own mini bar and pool table."
The party was busying up, but Jack was still happy to play good host to his cousin's colleagues.

"Spots or stripes boys?" asked Jack as he struck the triangle, potting one of each colour. "Oh, there's a drink on the side for you there Gimli"
"Cheers Jack" replied Kevin, whose brow had begun to sweat a little.
Jack messed up his follow-up shot and so he handed the cue to Mike whilst Kevin swilled his fine bourbon. It had been a while since Mike had played pool, but he used to play regularly with the football lads at the pub, so his game was solid enough.
"Nice work on the costume by the way Kevin," said Jack as Mike was lining up his first shot of the game, "I'm a big fan of the Peter Jackson movies."
Mike shut out their conversation and concentrated his focus. The nicotine and whiskey slipped into his bloodstream as his temples pulsated. He closed his left eye, and used his right to stare down the cue. He was Michael aiming his M4 assault rifle. He cocked back his weapon and pulled the trigger at his blue and white striped target. His aim was true and the connection sweet. But he had left himself nothing on. Mike always forgot to cover his tracks in this game. So he loosened his tie, undid his top button and smashed his second shot into a cluster of different balls. The impact was loud but he didn't pot again. As he looked up to pass Jack back his cue, he edged back towards his stool at the bar and admired the room once more.
"*Raging Bull*, *Kill Bill*, *Casino*, *Django*; you seem to like Martin and Quentin" Mike observed, feeling a bit more relaxed.
"Yeah, you could say that" replied Jack, striking another spot across the smooth green carpet, "Scorsese is, and always will be the King of Gangster flicks and well, Tarantino is just a genius auteur."

Mike stared at the *Casino* movie poster. The shiny red die drew his attention as the slogan jumped out at him:
Luck has nothing to do with the games they play
"Which is your favourite Tarantino?" Kevin asked Jack as he took his own first shot.
"*Reservoir Dogs* of course" said Jack, "why do you think I am dressed up as..."
"Mr Blonde" interjected Mike, "I knew that was who you were."
Jack approached Mike and slapped him on the thigh,
"My man" he beamed, "do you like Dogs too? Blonde your favourite?"
"I think I prefer Pink" replied Mike, "I'm a sucker for Buscemi"
"And is that who you're supposed to be tonight?"
"No, truth is I was stuck for ideas so I just played it safe with a suit. I guess I'm James Bond or Bruce Wayne or something"
Jack gave Mike a wink of approval.
"I've never seen *Reservoir Dogs* but I quite like *Inglorious Bastards*" said Kevin, passing Jack the cue and knocking back his bourbon.
"No way, you have a jukebox!" exclaimed Mike, falling deeper into love with Jack's man cave. "Does it work?"
"Sure does" said Jack, "let me just turn it on."

Chapter 26

The three men swayed to the soothing sounds of Sinatra as they swilled more bourbon. The cave had illuminated into a party within itself. Voice-boxes vibrated as the iced liquor tickled their tonsils. Mike felt his body loosen like a tie knot after a long day at work.

"I've got another surprise for you fellas" suggested Jack, who was thoroughly feeding off Mike and Kevin's enjoyment.

"Whatever next?" asked Kevin as Mike attempted to imitate Frank's tones. Jack slipped back behind the minibar, reached down and pulled gently on the brass handle of a drawer. He removed a small wooden casket and placed it on top of the bar.

"These, my friends," he said, gently lifting the lid, "are nineteen twenty-six fine blend cigars. I bought them in Cuba"

"Ha!" said Kevin, "us Dwarves are partial to an occasional smoke." He smacked his chest and held a stern face. Mike was impressed by Kev's dedication to the fancy dress theme.

"Well tonight's an occasion fellas," replied Jack, removing three cigars from the casket of eight, "come on, Tina and Dawn still aren't here. Lets go out back and feel like a couple of gangsters."

The boys left Sinatra playing as they exited the cave and head through to the kitchen. There were a few alcohol bottles dotted around but aside from those the kitchen was immaculate. Pop music played down the corridor from the living room. A sound which locked out as Kevin closed the back kitchen door behind them. Just as Mike was patting down his pockets, Jack pulled out a chrome Zipper lighter.

‘Everything he does is smooth’ thought Mike, 'no wonder he's related to Tina'.
The tip of Mike's cigar sizzled, crackled, glowed a bright red as he was sparked up. He held the smoke in his mouth before bellowing it out with controlled focus.
"I like you Jack" he said, the truth beginning to spill like the corner-shop bourbon.
"Well I like you fellas too. You know, back in Philly, and don't get me wrong I love Philly, but the nightlife wasn't quite the same. I mean, what can I say? I love England and the British girls are like....wow, ya feel me?"
'What about American girls?' thought Mike, nodding in agreement with what Jack said. Really, it was no different to what he had been doing all night. Kevin spluttered. The coughs came out all hoarse and throaty. Mike patted him on the back whilst Jack looked up at the stars. The rain had stopped, so the outdoor air was fresh and clear to pour out the three funnels of foggy tobacco smoke.

Mike made the decision to be a truly good friend by offering to help Kevin find the toilet. Kevin's coughing fit hadn't reacted too well with his alcohol consumption, which had forced him to produce a small mouthful of bile out in the back yard.
"It's just up here Kev mate"
"What?" grumbled Kev in response,
Mike looked back down the stairs at his friend. He couldn't help but laugh. A red faced, drunken dwarven warrior was bumbling up the stairs at 34 Highgate Avenue. His platted beard was still in tact, his battleaxe rested by the front door, but a small patch of sick was slowly sliding down his leather torso.
"The bathroom you dick" laughed Mike, "christ what a sight you look matey".

There were two upstairs bathrooms, both of which were crystal clean. An aroma of cinnamon squirted out of a self-timed plastic thing as Mike locked the door and dropped his trousers.
"Aaaaahhhhhhhhh" he let out as the urine impacted the toilet water. Mike's mind wandered back to Kev and he chuckled. Where the fuck were they? He twisted his neck to see an image of himself in the mirror which hugged the wall. He looked alright, aside from the fact that he was having a piss.
DING DONG
The front door bell rang and the house made a cheer. One about the size of a large dinner party. Mike could hear footsteps scurrying out of the living room, the twist of a lock, and then the door roar open.
"We're baaaack!"
The American tones of the arrivals came across like a Hollywood frat party movie. Yet Mike was still pissing like a racehorse and all the cheers and the I've-not-seen-you-in-ages screams had thrown him off. Yellowish whiskey piss splashed up against the side of the bowl. He pulled his penis the opposite direction but miscalculated as the warm piss splashed on the floor.
"Fuck" he said, putting it away and zipping up his fly. A tiny dribble of excitement slipped out to create a damp patch on his Calvin Kleins.
"Fuck" he said again. Unravelling the toilet roll as fast as he could he dabbed the floor and flushed the toilet.
'God I feel like Toby' he thought, 'I can't believe I just pissed on Tina's floor.'
Looking in the mirror, Mike felt a sudden rush of excited nerves. He'd almost forgotten about Tina over the last hour

of Gentlemanly fun with Jack and Kevin. Now here she was. Downstairs with her sister.

He ran his hand through his hair. That customary male sweep-to-one-side. He could hear Tina laughing downstairs. The belle of the ball.

'I wonder if she knows we are here yet?'

He fidgeted, pulled at his jacket sleeves, tightened a loose shirt button. This was it now. The time to shine. No fucking Ian, no Babs or Carol or that wanker Hardy giving him a grilling. No, it was just Mike, a loose Kevin, a clean cut Jacky boy and Tina. Sexy Tina who had invited him personally to the party. Mike knew what he had to do. His mind flashed like an old screen-roll. Chris, the money, the PlayStation, Sharon, Richie, Steph, Tony, Michael.

He readjusted his vision, slitted his eyes, truly focused on his reflection. He knew then that her devilish stare, her enticing smile would be too much for Mike to handle. He needed Michael's confidence, Michael's charisma. He also needed to get out of the fucking bathroom.

The door flew open and he caught it before it slammed against the wall. It had busied up downstairs since he and Kevin had arrived. So Mike sprang down the stairs sliding his hand down the bannister. The lounge had doubled, if not tripled in number and Mike could see the *Avatar* girls fussing over one another. He didn't want to give the impression of being desperate to see Tina. No, in his world it was cooler to act nonchalant. He strode past the living room and dipped into Jack's cave. Frank Sinatra had changed to Chic, and party vibrations tickled the atmosphere. That's when he saw her. He hadn't been expecting Tina in this room but there she sat, perched on the near side of the pool table. A butterfly traversed the dark pit of his stomach, so he felt the urge to drown the

winged-beast in whiskey. Unbeknown to him, time slowed. Everyone in the room moved at reduced speed. Jack was mixing up cocktails, shaking up liquids and laughing behind the bar, but everything else was a blur. Tina rested in a shiny leather jumpsuit, with long, black seductive leather stilettos. She too was laughing, as her arms supported her arched back to give the image of a foreign swan. Her hair curled, circled and rested effortlessly. Clouds of beautiful brunette ripples begging to be touched. Her dark porcelain skin were as soft as a doe, and that beauty spot on her left cheek stared Mike right in the eye.
"Michael!" she said, somewhat excitedly,
"Where have you been? Come here", she opened her arms and gently elevated herself from the billiards table, "have you been having fun?"
"I-we, erm, Kevin and I have been spending some good time with your cousin Jack" he managed to finally pull together, accepting the warmth of her embrace. Tina's hug was short but memorable. Mike could feel her hands gently grip his back muscles. He himself used a one arm hug. Casual, but with an intentional brush of her neck with the tip of his right index finger. Touching silk.
"I'm glad Jack has been keeping you company. Come here quick," she said, grabbing him by the hand and heading towards the door, "you have to meet my sister Dawn."
Time distorted within itself as Tina led Mike next door into the living room. She carried herself with such a relaxed confidence. Mike followed attached to her hand, conscious of looking charismatic rather than some hunched slave of hers. A simple readjusting of his shoulders and a lift of his closely-shaved chin did the trick.
"Dawn this is," Tina squeezed Mike's hand a little, "Mark."

Mike looked Tina in the face. She smiled that smile.
"I mean........Michael." The words elegantly escaped her cherry red lips. She continued, "Michael this is my dorky sister Dawn, dressed up as the seductive Poison Ivy. So don't kiss those lips", she said, before turning to a whisper, "they're venomous."
"It won't harm to kiss her hand then" said Mike, but upon turning around Tina was gone. Mike twisted his head back to Dawn.
"She vanished" smiled Dawn.
"Jesus, you sound exactly the same as her" said Mike, noticing that the smile wasn't quite the same.
"Ha! Most people say that. We're actually pretty different though."
Dawn had shorter hair than Tina and was slightly paler skinned. Over the course of their sofa conversation, Mike had begun to gather that she was two years younger than Tina, incredibly close to her cousin Jack, she worked in an organic juice bar and she was a carefree vegetarian.
"Yeah.....Tina gorges on cheeseburgers and stuff, which for me is kinda gross." Her glittery purple lips shimmered.
"Your costume is amazing" was all Mike could muster. Dawn wore a vibrant green jumpsuit which fitted her petite frame with perfection.
"Have you met my friend Kev?"
"No I didn't know you came with a friend. Tina only mentioned you."
'What might that mean?' thought Mike, spotting Kevin talking to Captain Jack and a bunch of Stormtroopers.
"Come on I'll introduce you.............GIMLI!" shouted Mike across the living room. It must have been loud because conversations stopped briefly and Mike could feel strangers' eyes on him. Maybe he was drunk?

Kevin swaggered over, all bubbly and alive.
"What have we here then? An Elf? A mermaid?" He grumbled, in character.
"A super villain" replied Dawn.

Mike was trapped in limbo between seeking out Tina and avoiding her to hide any interest. The party was filling up, the music was louder, the atmosphere loaded with excitement. Bright coloured costumes, beautiful girls, strange geeky fanboys and a smell of alcohol and tobacco smoke. Mike was a wandering cloud, a greyish white presence. Then he heard a, "Mikey boy."
It was a whisper and it was Jack.
"Here take this and follow me." Mike was handed a tumbler of bourbon and ice, and he felt obliged to follow Jack up the laminate stairs.
"Where we goin' mate?" he asked.
"Just follow me" said Jack, who walked into the toilet that Kev had been in. The pair of them had to shuffle past *Avatar* Clara, who had evidently just been topping up her make-up. This bathroom had a vanilla odour which Mike pointed out as Jack locked the door.
"You ain't nervous are ya?" joked Jack.
"For what?"
"This" said Jack, slipping a small square see-through sealy bag out of his dinner jacket pocket.
"What's that?"
"Cocaine bro. I figured you'd be cool with it."
"Does-"
"No. No-one knows Mikey. It's a boys secret"
"And Kev?"
"Come on bro, that dude is totally fucked up already."
There it lay. In the centre of Jack's palm. It was roughly a gram of tiny white dusty shards. Its had been years and

years since Mike had done some Coke. One of his old footy mates had been partial to a "Super Sunday". He thought of Sharon for the first time that night, and what she would think. He knew that she would strongly disagree. She thought it was a disgusting drug. Jack opened the red seal and dabbed some powder out into the groove between his thumb and his index. He took a large snort as Mike watched and thought,
'What would Michael do?'

Chapter 27

As Mike sneezed his way back down the stairs he knocked back his bourbon allowing the two shrunken ice cubes to slip into each other. Jack shuffled past as he did this and tapped his nose twice to reiterate the secret. Mike strolled into the lounge casually to see that a few people had begun to leave. Jack Sparrow still fumbled around asking everyone if they wanted some of his Captain Morgan's, and the *Avatar* girls still giggled amongst each other. All in all the atmosphere was a little less jubilant than before, but the party remained in full swing.
'I'll go for a fag' flashed Mike's mind as he span around out of the room and into the cave, nearly knocking into a rather tall, black, muscular Vampire.
"I will drink your blood" said the man, eyeballing Mike, to which Mike felt the need to apologise and stagger past.
'Who the fuck was that geezer?' he thought, sparking up a Marlboro.

The cave tumbled as Mike cracked his neck. Jack was playing pool against a helmet-less Stormtrooper, and Kevin was slumped in one corner, surrounded by Dawn and Tina. They were all laughing. Mike's eyes magnetised to Tina's arse, which fitted so tightly into her latex outfit, which was reflecting the colourful jukebox lights. Although the sisters had their backs to him and their attention on his mate, a voice commanded Mike look away and so he drifted his attention back to Jack's *Casino* poster. He met with Stone's eyes, followed by the seriousness of Pesci's and De Niro's. They followed him. Then there was the dice. That crystal red and white and then SNAP.
"Arghh Fuck!" shouted Mike as something sharp wrapped his hand causing a reflex action that dropped the cigarette.

"Where have you been? Why haven't you offered me a cigarette?"
It was a leather clad Tina walking towards him, gracefully feline.
"What did you just do?" asked Mike, who refused to look at his hand which was searing with pain. That's when he saw it, the thin long leathery whip which eloquently balanced in Tina's right hand. The end trailed the floor behind her.
"It's time we all got into character" she whispered into his ear, stubbing out the Marlboro with her stiletto, "and I don't know a thing about you."
The cocaine rolled up out of Mike's nose to his brain. His heartbeat sped, the 50s jazz swing amplified in his eardrums. He could see Tina continuing to seduce him. Her mouth purred at him but he was unconscious to the sounds of her words.

The cold crisp air soothed the sweat of his brow. Tina had taken him outside to the back yard. Two half smoked cigars still rested in a dry patch on the floor. She offered Mike a Camel.
"Have you got a light..........Catwoman?"
"That's the spirit.........."
Tina paused, which gave Mike a perfect cue to say something smart. He wanted to say "Bond, James Bond" but it was way too cliché. He thought about Michael but was unsure of his last name, so he eventually opted for, "Bruce Wayne of Wayne Manor."
The words came out calmly as the nicotine hit his throat. Tina continued,
"Oh Mr Wayne. I had no idea you were Gotham's Dark Knight." She stared, then smiled and broke character. She was, in truth, a little drunk. Tina stroked her hand down

Mike's chest, the cigarette smoke masking her caramel complexion. Her red lips shone like the die on the poster.

"So, what do you think of my sister?"

"She seems cool. She has lighter skin than you though, right? I mean, you're both half-caste— I mean, mixed race but—"

Tina pressed her index finger to his lips. Silencing him.

"No Michael I don't think you're racist. You should relax you know. Try to be more like Kevin."

This was a blow to the gut.

"Kevin?"

"Yeah he's awesome. I'm so glad you brought him. I was just talking to him about Batman villains— hence mine and my sister's costumes— and we were talking about who plays the best Joker. I'm torn between Jack Nicholson and Heath Ledger but Kevin told me his favourite was Mark Hamill, who voiced Joker in some animated game or something.

"I knew you would like him" said Mike, "but how curious that I should be your caped crusader at this party?"

Mike looked Tina deep in her eyes. They smiled so slightly. Mike's head was a roulette table, spinning black, red, black, green until he shook out of it. There it lay, that small delicate dainty freckle. Just on her cheek above her lip.

"I like your freckle." It just came out. Mike brushed it with his fingertip as Tina gently tilted her head, exposing her neck.

"You're mysterious Master Wayne" she said, taking a toke of her cigarette, "and it's actually a beauty spot." She smiled that flirtatious smile.

Mike was about to say something. He didn't know what. His mind flashed back to the first cigarette they shared

together on their work break. He opened his mouth but Tina spoke first. The words came slow with conviction.
"Sometimes you can trust in someone better when you know nothing about them."
The pair gravitated towards one another as their lips locked. Mike stiffened as she pressed her body close against his. He could smell her hair, her soft skin. A creamy cocoa butter.

Kevin was trashed. Slumped in the corner, staring. Tina floated off to find her sister as Jack serenaded the remaining guests. Mike looked at the time. It was twenty-to-four.
"P-p-please tell me it's time to go home" gargled Kevin through his fake redwood beard. Mike laughed,
"Sure thing mate I'll call a taxi for us now."

Smoke and Mirrors

They say that home is where the heart is Michael.

Yeah, I know. But what are you getting at Doc?

Well, I guess I'm curious as to how much quality time you spend at your house in the Hills. Time with your wife and your children.

Truth is not a lot. I spend a lot more time inside my own head. I mean when I am not sleeping with nightmares I am living through danger. I care about her, and the kids too, but I am convinced she is sharing other guys' beds, and well, the clouded honesty in our marriage leads me directly to the smoke and mirrors of strip-joints.

Does your wife know about these visits? After all, studies have shown that happiness is built upon strong and healthy relationships. Those relationships are typically built around one thing. Trust.

Trust? Ha! If God has taught me one thing in this meaningless life of mine, it's to never trust a soul. Let me tell you something Doc, this is a dog-eat-dog world. People will trample all over you to get what they want. You're either a wolf, a sheep, or a wolf in sheep's clothing.

So then, what are you?

I'm whatever God chooses me to be, which is usually the meanest, most deceiving wolf in the lands. Which brings me back around to my story. It was early evening, the sky drizzled. I'd been watching some movie where the lead actor kept fucking all these women. It wasn't a porno, it was this prohibition-era gangster flick, right? Anyways it got me feeling in the mood. The other half was out at this tennis tournament further up in the hills somewhere, and the kids were at her moms for the night. I'd just raked in a nice little earner due to this informant of mine that keeps himself busy around the auto garages near South Central. His kinda work is usually centred around gang friction and drug territory, but this had been an easy pay check. Mere protection during a transfer of silenced machine pistols from one of the Mexican gangs to one of the many Black gangs in the local area. That job really was a piece of cake. So..... I decided to take my earnings to Hookers.

Hookers? I'm not familiar with the place.

I told you Doc. It's a strip-club. A place where all the sleaze, smut and scum in this town go to seek out some adult pleasure. I gotta say this place is practically the opposite of "truth". This is sweat, smoke and secrecy. This place is pure sleaziness.

Sounds lovely.

It really isn't. It's an awful place but the girls are foxes. Julia was out on the pole, scantily clad. She caught my attention as soon as I entered. I was wearing my shades and a powder grey suit, so you could say I looked a little smarter than the other clientele. Julia though, she was new. A devil she is. She's got brunette hair pulled back, with a tiny peace symbol tattooed behind her ear. A real minx. I told the bartender to get me a drink and walked towards the rail for a closer look. My god the way this girl was moving. Her underwear was bright red and it sat so perfectly on her beautiful body. There were a coupla other guys staring at her but her attention was all on me. So I started flicking dollar bills at her. At first, single notes, but it wasn't long till I was making it rain. Once she got off the stage, she took me for a private dance in one of the back rooms. Pressing her tits against my face she was. It didn't take her long to suggest that we go back to her place.

So, I'm confused. Are these girls dancers or prostitutes?

Like with most shit the line is blurred Doc. All I know is she knew I had money. So I met her round the back of the strip-joint. She'd put a fur coat on over her underwear and I remember her calling me a "nice guy" as we got into my car. I drove a coupla blocks, all the while thinking about what I would do to her.

And your wife? Were you thinking about her? About her tennis competition?

Of course not Doc stop ruining the fucking story. The only thing my wife cares about is me not getting fucking killed. Now, where were we? Oh yeah, so I get back to hers and park up outside her apartment. This is a sketchy neighbourhood I'm talking about. Out of service street lights, occasional gun shot noises and pit-bulls barking. I took her inside and fucked her like crazy, but here's the thing. During it all I got a call on my cell from that informant I told you about. "They're onto you" he told me. Apparently some dude in Hookers had spotted me being frivolous with my money and had recognised me from the gun transfer job.

Wow! So, what happened Michael?

What happened!? I heard tyres screeching round the corner and told Julia to get the fuck down on the deck. These gang-banging motherfuckers don't mess around. They must have wound the window down and leaned out because a barrage of buckets chewed through the wall of Julia's apartment. My heart was beating pretty quickly. I had that feeling of being caught out you know. I pulled out my rubber grip and took a few shots back at them. Blind-firing out the broken glass window. These fuckers started to drive off, so I apologised to and thanked Julia, then ran outside to see if I could chase them. They had fucked my car up real bad. My night too.

Oh, my oh my is that the time? Sorry Michael but we've exceeded our allocated time. I'll add the time to your next bill if you don't mind. And remember, no session next week as I am on vacation.

Yeah, I remember. Have a good one and see ya next time Doc.

Chapter 28

Mike woke before Kevin on Saturday morning. He'd stayed over at Kevin's flat after deciding enough was enough during the taxi ride home. Kevin was snoring loudly in his bed as Mike wrestled around amongst computer cables, instruction manuals and fantasy action figures. 'It was only a kiss' he thought.

The time was ten to ten and birds were tweeting outside in the late morning sunshine. He cracked his neck, stretched his eyes and then closed tight. His head buzzed. 'Must be all that whiskey'. Kevin snored. Then snored again. And again, exactly like the clockwork of a beaten dwarven warrior. Posters upon posters littered the walls and ceiling. Literally everything from *Alien* and *The Matrix* to Stanley Kubrick films and Vince Gilligan series'. Mike rolled over onto his left side, clutching the hagged sleeping bag like a ten year old boy. His mouth was dry. His bladder was full. O, how he wished someone would take care of him right now.

'Sharon! My phone? Shit. I've got to get my shit together.' Mike tossed and turned over onto his right side. His pelvis felt so hard against the carpeted floor. He kept his eyes closed and let his mind wander. Although Kev's snore was tough to keep out, the chirrups of those sweet birds came to the foreground of his mind. Mike couldn't decide if he was hungover or still pissed. Either way it didn't matter. He had no choice.

'We were only being friendly'

'Yeah and she looked so hot'

'I wonder who knows?'

'I bet even Kevin doesn't know'

'Jack'll know. For sure. And Dawn.'

'God it was so good though'
'It was only a kiss.'

When Mike next awoke it was eleven thirty. He'd drifted back off and an hour and a half had slipped by. "Right. Phone" he said, almost loud enough to help wake Kev up. He escaped the sleeping bag and surveyed the room for his belongings. His suit hung over the back of Kevin's computer chair, creased, drink stained and stinking of smoke. Kevin was still sleeping, but his eyes were almost half open, like he was observing Mike through a magical trance. Mike waved his hand in front just to check. Kevin was still out for the count. Luckily, Mike's phone rested in the inside pocket of his suit jacket. He thanked God he hadn't lost it. A God he didn't necessarily believe in. He pressed a few buttons.
"Fuck. No fucking battery. Shit"
He felt in the mood to swear and curse. It was hot and stuffy in Kevin's bedroom. Finding a phone charger was proving a difficult task amongst the debris and chaos caused by Kevin's computer virus. Mike sifted through the black power cables, USB leads, aux wires and instruction manuals until he saw one that he thought would work. He quickly plugged it in near Kevin's bedside table and took the liberty of going for a quick shower.

As he stood upright in the bathtub, naked and fragile, the water escaped the shower head. It was so cold it gave him goosebumps. He twisted the tap to be greeted by the antithesis. Boiling hot water scolding to the touch. It took him some time to find an acceptable temperature until he gave up and grabbed one of the three smelly towels. Back in the bedroom, Kevin had woken up.
"Good morning Master Bruce" he said in his best Albert impression, "did you have a pleasant evening?"

The two laughed as Mike went to look at his phone.
"You were so funny last night Kev"
"Was I? I don't remember too much"
"Sign of a good night I say"
"Aye" replied Kevin, "D'ya want a brew?"
"Coffee if you have it" said Mike.

Two missed called and three text messages. One of the calls was from Kevin, the other from an unknown number he didn't have in his phonebook. Two of the written messages were from Sharon, and they read as follows:

Hey baby hope you have a good night with your old footy friends. Sorry if I've been a little argumentative recently. U know that I love u. Be safe x (sent at 21:47)

Mike, I know u told me u had a bit of a football weekend planned, and I don't want to be a nag, but T + S have asked us over 4 dinner tnyt. I know it's not ideal but given the circumstances I think we should go. Msg me back so I know you're safe. Love u, S x (Sent at 08:55)

The third message was from Chris, asking about meeting at the pub again soon. Mike sent no replies, allowing his phone to gather more charge. He waited for his coffee.
"So, did anything happen with you know who?" asked Kevin, who strutted back into his electrical bomb site with two cups of regular black coffee. "Sorry we've got no milk or sugar"
"No worries" responded Mike, settling for his bitter black cup of joe. He thought of his response, then figured he needed to avoid petty lies at any given opportunity. They spoke about Jack, Tina, Dawn, the *Avatar* girls and that creepy fella dressed up as Johnny Depp.

"It was only one kiss though" Mike repeated.
"Yeah" replied Kevin.
"Listen Kev, you know as well as I do that Shaz doesn't know anything about last night. So, please can we keep it that way?"
Kevin reassured him and in return Mike offered to help Kev tidy his room.

Mike pulled his sticky suit back on and left Kevin's flat around half past twelve. As he waited for his taxi, an angular looking blackbird peered at him and called him names. The taxi driver was quiet and professional, exactly what Mike needed as he mulled things over. He replied to Chris letting him know that he'd been busy but they would meet up soon. Then he sent a message to his wife.

Morning baby, sorry I've been out of reach. My phone was out of battery and the lads didn't have the right charger. Tnyt sounds good, I'll be home soon, M x

Still coming round and feeling a little agitated, he checked his pockets for the usual: wallet, phone, keys. He had them all, but then he remembered his Grandfather's stag flask. Where was it? He hadn't seen it at Kevin's. Instinctively his thumb directed him to that unknown missed call number and he hit green.
"Hello?"
"Hi, uhm, this is Mike from last night"
"Mikey boy! My man! It's Jack, everything good bro? Did you have fun last night?"
"Fun? Yeah, of course, thanks for your hospitality. Kev and I had a great time"
"Sure thing bro, sure thing"

"Hey listen, you didn't happen to come across a silver hip flash did you? I think I might have left it at the party"
"You're in luck buddy, I've got it right here. Swing over now if you want and grab it. Dawn and I are just playing a little *Tekken* if you fancy getting your ass kicked!?"
"PlayStation or Xbox?" asked Mike, "I mean, what am I saying? I can't right now. I've got an appointment"
"Y'all good, I'll just.......wait, one second........Ha! I fucking countered that shit Dawn....uhm, yeah sorry no problems dude. I'll just give it to Tina and she can give it you in work on Monday I guess."
Mike could tell he didn't have Jack's full attention so he simply agreed with what he was saying, thanked him again for a great night and hung up. He thought of Tina. A tipsy, provocative Tina who handled a whip.
"A fucking whip" he muttered in disbelief, to which the driver responded,
"U wat mate?"
"Aaah nothin' mate," replied Mike looking at the red mark on his hand. In his mind there was no time to be wasted finding out about this fella's life. Taxi drivers always pour their hearts out to a solo passenger.

An email appeared on his smart phone. It was from Bet a'Luck. It had completely slipped his mind that in the midst of his football weekend lie to Sharon, Mike had actually put an accumulator on. Better still he was off to a good start after guessing the Friday night kick off would be one-nil win to the away team.
"Hmph" he produced, 'only another seven results to get right' he thought. The odds were against him anyway he thought, sitting there hungover in the back of a smelly taxi on his way to an NCP carpark to pick up his car and yesterday's work clothes. His car was there, untouched. The

taxi driver bid Mike a good day and for the first time since Highgate Avenue, Mike was truly alone. It was a good job really, because he had to get changed in the backseat of his car for the second time in twenty-four hours. It was such an awkward thing to do whilst hungover that he quickly grew impatient and then angry.
"FUCK" he shouted, slamming his palm against the roof.
Eventually, he got in the driver's seat, realigned his belt, turned the key and set off home.

Chapter 29

The house was quiet once Mike arrived home. Sharon's car was nowhere to be seen and she'd left no note. Toby slept heavily in his bed and Mike gave him a gentle stroke before stripping and throwing his work clothes in the washing machine. He had left his suit in the boot of his car which he knew he needed to take to the Dry-Cleaners. The house was spotless, Sharon must have been cleaning. A small pang of guilt surged through Mike, as he imagined Sharon ironing, mopping and dusting alone at home last night. With nothing imperative to do, he went and sat down in his trusty chair.

"Ahhhhhh, yes that feels good" he said, discovering a box of cigarettes on the side table.

"Menthol?" 'Wait, has Shaz started on the ciggies?' Nevertheless he sparked one up and fired up Chris' PlayStation. He selected the first-person mode for ultimate immersion, with the intention (he thought, taking a cool pull from the minty cigarette) of going on a complete rampage and killing a load of cops and civilians.

Michael was at his luxury home, sat watching a movie with his complaining teenage children. He walked into the kitchen and took a shot of whiskey, the calm before the storm. A black stolen Comet was parked in the garage and Michael shouted a "Daddy's leaving" as he got in. He turned the radio on and drove slowly out, down the path towards the automatic gate which opened him up to the world. He swung the car left, pressed the gas and revved down the road into Hollywood. There were always some types of lunatics there, so that's where he headed. Cruising down the boulevard an array of fancy sports cars shifted lanes on their way towards Rockford Hills. Michael weaved in and out and in between any vehicle that crossed his path, when a ninja bike cut in front of him. The bike smashed against his windshield and the driver was forced a few metres through the air before impacting abruptly with the concrete road. This was just the trigger he needed. A few women with nice handbags and designer sunglasses let out piercing shrieks at what had occurred, so Michael unloaded his TEC-9 out of the window with bullets hitting numerous pedestrians. Injured and bleeding on the floor, blood spread over the Hollywood stars as sirens sounded in the distance. The tyres screeched as the rubber burnt the road and Michael sped off from the scene. He made a right, heading south down one of the many freeways. The sun bleached the road and bounced off shiny metallic supercars. A cop car appeared in Michael's eyeline, driving at a steady speed a few vehicles in front of his speeding Comet. Mike could have chosen to spin his car around but he fancied the buzz. So, he swapped weapons to a combat pistol and started firing shots straight through the front windscreen. The glass smashed after four shots and many cars on the freeway veered off to one side. One of the bullets hit the back left tyre of the police car causing it to spin like an off balance ice-skater. Perpendicular to Michael's car, the two officers looked out their car door window, straight at him. Two more direct bullets split their heads like coconuts. The inside of the patrol car an image from a slaughterhouse. Mike press his foot flat down on his accelerator once he heard the sirens double. They pierced his eardrums like bullets through flesh. Now he wasn't slowing down for anything. A speeding bullet train zipping through the intersection. Police vehicles parked up in a line ahead of him, blocking the road off. Michael took the approaching exit and came out just near the South Central area.

Gangland territory. A radio advert spoke to him about finding the truth. Some sort of cult program. So he flicked to West Coast classics to try and fit in with the street corner clusters of Purple, Green and Yellow.
"Sup homie?" shouted a gangbanger, which pissed him off. Mike got out of the car and approached the hustler.
"How do you like this?" said Mike, wielding a metal baseball bat. He cracked the bat around the hustler's head. A home run. G Funk merged with the sirens as a whole clique of black gangsters emerged from the side of a chicken restaurant. So Michael crouched down behind his car and re-equipped his handgun. The gang fired shots at him. Bullet ripped through the Comet. In between clips he would respond, taking aim at their heads and torsos. A few of the hustlers' bullets hit him as two police bikes skidded around the corner to the early evening crossfire. If he wasn't careful this could be the end.

Evidently the police officers knew they were outnumbered by an array of street weapons. They must have radioed back-up because a helicopter soon swooped over the area. It was time for Mike to get the fuck out of there. So he ran. He kept running, off the main road towards the residential area. The motorcyclists pursued him, as did the remaining gangstas who were still coming to terms with their homies who lay dead on the concrete.
"I should have brought some body armour" Michael said, before seeing a bright orange muscle car pull up at a red light. He sprinted towards the car, opened the driver's side door and pistol-whipped the male driver who screamed in pain as the butt of the gun cracked his forehead. Bullets flew in Michael's direction as he commandeered the vehicle. Some washed up radio host was talking about how much blow he did in the 80s and 90s. Two police officers

took aim out the side doors of the chopper. They fired their assault rifles and Michael tried to fire back whilst driving. What with the angle and the speed and the weight of the muscle car, he smashed it into the side of a truck. Things were getting out of hand so he headed onto the train tracks to try and avoid anymore collisions. He leaned out the car window, pulled the pin and then dropped a grenade on the floor. He kept driving towards a tunnel before looking back at the insane explosion of two LCPD cars. Flames licked the sky and thick black smog erupted like a volcano. Mike was laughing until he spun back around to see a large freight train heading directly towards him. He had split-seconds to react or accept his fate. The train driver sounded his powerful airhorn as Michael pulled hard left on the steering wheel, avoiding the head on collision by the skin of his teeth.

He paused the game as the sound of the front door key lock turned.

"Oh hi honey" smiled Sharon, "how are you?" She approached him and gave him a kiss. She looked beautiful with her make-up perfectly done, but there was an underlying concern in the creases of her mouth.

Mike's phone beeped.

"Are you alright Shaz? You look gorgeous by the way." He peeked at his phone screen and it was a short message from an unknown number.

"Aww thanks honey" she said, taking a menthol out of the box. Mike read the message quickly before clicking the stand-by button on his phone.

I had such a great time last night. Jack told me about your hip-flask. Don't worry it's in safe hands, T x

"It's just this meal this evening. Steph is so concerned about Tony. I think their marriage is truly on the rocks."
Mike wasn't really listening.
"Well, we'll just have to see what happens."
"Yeah," Sharon said, pulling on her cigarette, "anyway, come on you. Turn your game off and go and get changed."
"Have you started smoking again?"
"No" she said, exhaling smoke, "this is just a one off."
"I'm not judging don't worry" said her husband, turning off the PlayStation. "I'll go and get ready now."

Chapter 30

They arrived at the Marigold around seven-thirty. The taxi ride had been quiet. Sharon was on her phone messaging Steph. Mike was thinking; constantly thinking about Tina. He just couldn't get the image of her out of his head. He convinced himself he didn't need to feel guilty for it was only a kiss.

'She was just being friendly' he kept thinking. 'It would have been rude to dismiss her kiss.'

He was so tempted to reply to her text message, but he couldn't just message Tina in front of his wife. Besides, it was temptation that had got him here in the first place. Mike had made his choices, firstly to go to the party, secondly to get blind drunk, thirdly to snort some cocaine with Jack, and finally to embrace Tina.

"Oh there they are" said Sharon, as they walked into the restaurant.

Tony was wearing a garish orange shirt with the top three buttons open like an Italian. Steph wore a tight flowery dress which accentuated her breasts. There was a slight distance between them at the table.

"Hi babes" beamed Steph upon seeing her sister, "hi Mike are you okay?"

"Mikey boyyyy!" cackled Tony, as might a feral hyena.

"Alright man" replied Mike, opening up to a handshake.

The sisters were talking about each others outfits.

"Man!? I ain't your man bro. You gotta get down to the gym buddy!"

Tony twisted the traditional handshake into a "homie" style hand clap, and let out a loud, single, fake laugh. Mike sat down and wanted to leave. Small talk proceeded until the

waiter interjected. A tall thin man with a large hooked nose and an air of grace.
"What can I get you to drink? Ladies?"
"Ooo, erm, a dry white wine please" said Sharon.
"And for me a glass of red" continued Steph.
"Gentlemen?"
"What whiskeys have you got?" asked Mike, but before the waiter could respond the hyena jumped in.
"Whiskey!? Hey big time! Ha! Mikey boyyyy."
Mike refused to respond in the slightest. He stared the whole time at the waiters eyes and nose.
"We have a large variety Sir. Scotch or Bourbon?"
"Just get me any of your Bourbons on the rocks."
"And I'll just have a beer" said Tony, "I'm not as cool as this guy."
The waiter gave a gentle nod and promised to be back shortly to take food orders. There was a brief moment of silence except for Tony sniffling.
"A whiskey Mike?" said Sharon, gently stroking the side of his face.
"Yeah, I just fancied one" he brushed off. Tony was on his smart phone.
"So, how's work Mike? Everything well?" asked Steph.
Mike couldn't tell if she was prying, or, being lovely like always.
"Yeah work's not bad. Same old. How's things with you?"
Tony looked to Steph for her reaction.
"Yeah we're alright aren't we" she said, looking at her husband.
"Have you eaten here before?" Sharon asked.
"Yeah it's probably the best chinky in town" replied Tony.
The Chinese abbreviation inappropriately bitter to digest.

The waiter returned with the drinks and Mike savoured his first cold sip of the brown liquid.
"Cheers" said Sharon, raising her glass to the group.
The couples ordered their food and the waiter scuttled off to the kitchen.
"Like I was saying, we can sort you both out with a couples membership to our gym can't we Ton'" said Steph. "It works out really cheap if one couple invites another."
Mike wasn't interested in joining a gym. Tony was back on his phone.
"I'm just going to pop to the toilet" Mike said standing up. His phone was burning in his pocket.

He opened the cubicle and slid his trousers down to his ankles. He couldn't believe it, another text from Tina.

Aren't you going to message me back, Mr Wayne.......?

A rush of excitement raced down his legs as the final stages of his digestive system kicked in. Some toilet water splashed against his hairy cheeks. He started to type,

I take it this is Tina..... Yeah I had a really good night thanks. Your sister and cousin were really friendly. Glad to hear my flask is in good hands, M

He hit send, then re-read what he had just written. He realised he hadn't asked any questions and had probably closed the conversation, but he was becoming conscious that he'd been gone from the table a while. So he cleaned up, washed his hands and looked at himself in the mirror. He almost stared through himself, rejigging his fragmented memory from the previous nights events.

There was an underlying tension back at the table. Tony was talking a little faster than usual and the sisters were just listening, analysing. A female Watson and Holmes.
"See that's the thing about investment," said Tony, "you're banking on yourself."
Mike gently nodded but didn't really understand the statement.
"But what about the risk factor?" asked Sharon, crossing her legs.
"You can cho-" Steph began to reply,
"That's down to the individual as well," commanded Tony.
"Depends on how big your bollocks are hey Mikey?" he laughed.
'I wish you would chew on a bollock' Mike thought, just as his phone vibrated in his pocket. The waiter returned with the noodle dishes and as he placed the food down, Mike took a quick peek at his phone to see Tina's reply. It wasn't her.
"Oh my god I don't fucking believe it" said Mike, probably a little loudly for his social surroundings.
Sharon could read the excitement on her husband's face.
"What? What is it Mike?"
Mike tilted his head back, closed his eyes and grinned like the Cheshire Cat. Suspense captured the table.
"Come on Mike tell us!" chirped Steph.
He opened his eyes.
"The football. I don't honestly believe it, I've won."
"Won what?" asked Sharon.
"That bet. I mean, I put an eight game accumulator on. I put it on Friday evening."
"Well?"

"I stuck twenty quid on and guessed win, draw or lose on eight different matches. They *all* came through!"
"How much have we won?" asked his wife excitedly.
"One thousand three hundred and ninety six pounds."

Chapter 31

The rest of the double dinner date went swimmingly for Mike. This completely unexpected news overshadowed his discomfort of sitting opposite his brother in law. Mike had insisted he bought everyone another round of drinks, and felt that feeling of giving a homeless man twenty quid. He knew his bet had been a cover story to fall in line with Friday night. It wasn't calculated at all, and this played on his mind as him and Sharon waved goodbye to Steph and Tony and jumped into the back of the black cab.
"The food was nice in there wasn't it" Sharon said, fastening her seatbelt. Mike was just staring out the window. She smiled. "You can't stop thinking about it can you?"
"I've never won anything like this"
"That's true"
"I've rotten luck usually"
"Well?"
"Someone up there must like me"
"Oh give over would ya," Sharon said giving him a kiss on his stubbly cheek, "what are we gonna spend the money on then? We could use it to help decorate the kitchen!"
But Mike was busy cooking up other plans. His brain was a travel brochure, flicking through pages of exotic and far-reaching holiday destinations.
"It's not *that* much money," he said, "but it's the perfect amount for a holiday."
He started to think about how he could make more money. Investing what he'd just earned or, placing even more accumulators.
Sharon's phone sounded.
"Oh I've just had a text from our Steph"

"Oh yeah?"
"Yeah and she's saying that what's happened with your bet has made her question things."
"About what?" answered Mike, shuffling into his seat.
Sharon looked round at the taxi driver who was concentrating on the road.
"About Tony. Remember she was thinking he had a gambling problem? Well she's asking me if I still think that's the case now. Something about his reaction."
"Well how did he react?" asked Mike.
"What do you mean Mike? He was sitting right in front of you!"
"I know but I can't stand to look at him. He's a twat!"
"Well, I think the problem is that he appeared, well, largely unaffected."
"Yeah I guess I know what you mean. I half-expected him to go really quiet or something"
"Yeah, or ask you a few questions about the bet. I mean, if he's got a gambling problem......"
"So, maybe he doesn't have a gambling problem"
"This is what I think Steph is getting at."
Mike's phone vibrated.
"There's something not right between them though isn't there. Could you feel how forced their conversations felt?"
Sharon looked concerned. Mike's phone vibrated again in his pocket. Sharon clutched her husband's large hands between her own soft angelic ones. Her eyes met his.
"We're okay aren't we Mike?"
It was a high speed curveball, straight and honest. He just needed to catch it.
"Yeah of course babe." He kissed her. It was his second guilty kiss of the weekend. Her eyes were like fishbowls

full of coral, colour and life. His eyes hid the truth this time. He was conscious of conveying the old Mike.

Sharon returned to her phone to reply to her sister after her husband's reassuring kiss. Mike pulled his phone out too. The first message was from the betting company, informing Mike that the funds would be deposited into his account in the next 24-48 hours. The second message was from her.

I hope you like surprises. I'll message you tomorrow....x

He didn't reply. There was no need to. He paid the driver, Sharon thanked him and then they walked up the driveway together.

"I'm going straight to bed I'm tired honey" she said unlocking the front door.

"Okay I'm just going to have a cup of tea and a fag. I won't be long"

They kissed each other goodnight.

"I love you"

"I love you.”

Toby was sleeping in his bed, making loud noises which pissed Mike off a little. He wandered over to the kettle, saw that there was still enough water in it and flicked the switch. The water began to bubble. Bubble and boil as Mike tossed a teabag into an empty mug. The rain started to patter against the window. He gazed out at the drizzled pavements whilst the kettle noises intensified. He re-read Tina's message, smiled in anticipation at her forthcoming contact then closed the curtains. The clear scolding water filled the mug and the tiny tea leaves absorbed it, drank it and copperised it. Mike stirred the drink, watching intently as the copper darkened and the bag sunk slowly. He grabbed the milk from the fridge and checked the date to see if it was still good. The milk slipstreamed the brew, and the dark bitterness was clouded over. Mike sipped his cup of tea and gazed into the hollow darkness of the fireplace. Allowing his frequent frantic thoughts to come and go as they pleased.

That night he drifted off peacefully on his side of the bed. Thoughts, forms, shadows and figures flitted in and out of the scene inside his mind. Mike's legs were rooted to the spot and the creamy infusion of the milk and tea transfixed his thoughts to a forested pathway. Richie was trudging slowly down the gravel. His hands buried deep inside his pockets, his hood covering his face. A thick linked rusted chain was attached to a circular clasp which wrapped around his ankle. Walking forward slackened the strain so that's what he continued to do. Trudge. One foot at a time, forwards but with his head bowed.
"Richie............Richie..........." Mike tried to shout, but the words couldn't escape his mouth. Richie walked straight past and made no acknowledgement of him. Mike's eyes followed him down the gravel path. The crunching of those dusty stones underfoot. The trees leaves sat so still in this cold misty scene. Step, step Richie advanced. Until a silhouette appeared in the distance of his very direction. There was someone walking towards him. Mike remained rooted as the two walking figures approached each other due to some force of nature. Then Richie stopped. The chain linking his leg to the other man's continued to slacken. Richie lifted his hood to reveal a sunken skull-like face. It turned abruptly and started to run back in the direction it had come from. Mike watched the sharp movement of Richie, and followed him running away from the approaching figure that revealed itself to be Richie's

father. The gaunt image of Richie slipped and the chain tautened. His face came crashing down and impacted the hard gravel. Mike gasped, sat up and removed his sweaty bed-shirt. Sharon continued to sleep angelically.

Chapter 32

Mike woke with a headache on Sunday morning. It was a subtle throb, not the searing, cold flannel type. Sharon had half opened the curtains and was sat up in bed reading a glossy magazine. The sky was grey and a slight breeze teased the drawn curtain.

"Morning babe" Mike said, rubbing his head.

"Good morning love, are you alright?"

"Yeah, I just........ I had a weird dream is all. And I've got a bit of a headache." Sharon kissed his forehead.

"Awww, what about love? I've got some ibuprofen downstairs if you want?"

"Nah, I better eat first" he said before falling silent and closing his eyes.

"So?" said his wife, "What was this dream about?"

"It was more of a nightmare" he replied. He opened his eyes and his vision took a few seconds to return. A cloudy dizziness.

"I can't really remember it. It was something about our Rich"

"Bless him. God knows how he's coping with that lousy father of his." It wasn't usual for Sharon to so openly disregard Tony.

"Maybe I should give him a call on his mobile. See how he is."

"You can do" said Sharon, spinning her legs out the side of the bed, "I'll go down and get you some toast, tablets and a brew."

"Cheers love" he replied, picking up the magazine she left on the bed. The women in the magazine were flawless. All their blemishes and imperfections had been erased or covered up. Make-up glittered and hair shimmered. There were plenty of stories about pregnancies, second-marriages and weight loss. Beautifully kempt couples smiled off the pages. A fragrance model with toffee skin caught Mike's eye. She was similar to Tina. He glanced at his phone but it was the usual home screen that stared back at him. He read Tina's message once more, then deleted it. He knew he needed to be very careful with that sort of thing. Sharon came back up with breakfast and Mike popped two ibuprofen tablets.

Three o'clock rolled by like an old steam engine and Mike had done nothing of significance with his day. He'd had lunch, watched a couple of quiz shows on the telly, discussed Steph and Tony again with Sharon, and phoned Chris. They arranged to meet on Tuesday after work at the pub.

"Bring my PlayStation with ya" Chris had said, "I've got ya money for ya."

Mike was growing impatient waiting for Tina to reveal her surprise. He must have secretly checked his phone about six or seven times and had received nothing except a message from Kev reminiscing about Friday night.

"Are you going to call then?" asked Sharon, going through all her old receipts.

"Who?"

"Richie. See how he is like?"

"Do ya think I should bother? I mean, I don't wanna stick my nose in do I?"

"Mike. You know that Rich loves talking to you. You don't judge him all the time like Tony does."

"I suppose" said Mike. "I'll phone him but not right now."

"Alright, well I'm just going to pop to the supermarket and get a few bits in. The cupboards are bare"

"Oh okay great. Will you make sure you get the thick smokey bacon I like?"
"Of course I will love" she said, kissing him, "best get packing that console up if Chris is saying he wants it back!"
"Yeah, I guess" said Mike as she closed the door behind herself and got in her car.

Mike had a fag and thought back to the fragments of his dream. He felt a feeling of trepidation and seriously wondered if Richie was alright. Clearly, he thought, Steph was now thinking that Tony was up to no good, and Mike wondered if Rich knew anymore about it than he or Sharon did. Mike phoned Richie's mobile. It went straight through to voicemail so he left an impromptu message.
"Hiya Rich it's your Uncle Mike. Did you hear the news about my uhm..... my win? Aaaaanyway I was thinking I could take you out for a burger sometime soon. There's this great place near my work. Hope you're good. Give me a ring back."
Then he hit red. He fired up Chris' console for a quick play around and had fun being chased by the police. In and around the city, out into the open country, Mike sang along as Michael controlled the wheel in the driving seat. Mike had just lit up another fag and pulled onto the open road North, when his phone buzzed. He immediately paused the game and read:

Friday at the party was fun and all that but there were a LOT of people there, right? Let's meet for a drink at seven-thirty. The Glass Hotel in the city centre. Come smart, T x

Chapter 33

It was approaching twenty-to-eight when Mike finally found a parking space at the Glass Hotel. He had wanted to leave the house whilst Sharon was still at the supermarket, so had left a note on the kitchen surface explaining that he had gone to Chris' place to drop off the PlayStation and catch up. The console rested in the boot of his car. The truth is, Mike might have had the time to drop off at Chris' before coming to meet Tina, but he didn't want his catch up with Chris to run on too long. He couldn't miss this window of opportunity. He was wearing a smart denim shirt with a buttoned down collar, and he had even found time to wipe down his smart shoes. His hair was clean, gelled and brushed, and a sophisticated cologne radiated from the pores of his wrists. Before he got out of his car he looked deep into his eyes through the reflection of the rear-view mirror.

The hotel bar was fairly busy. Bartenders in dicky bow-ties flirted with cocktail bottles; pouring, shaking and stirring mojitos and gin & tonics. Groups of businessmen laughed and drank at round tables and soft jazz emitted an ambience of sophistication. Tina was sitting alone in a corner booth, waiting for her work-mate. She was wearing all black, with touches of gold to complement her outfit. Pointed-toe shoes, tights and a sleek dark dress encrusted with tiny diamonds. Her legs were crossed and her right foot wagged like a puppy's tail, pointing towards Mike. As he walked confidently towards her, he focused on her top half. Her breasts so perfectly formed. Tina smiled and her rouge lipstick begged to be kissed like a medieval shrine. Her make-up was so expertly executed. The foundation layered with the soft strokes of blusher. Eyelashes thick and bold.

"What time do you call this Mister?"

Mike checked his watch. "Quarter to eight" he smiled.

"Exactly" she said as Mike sat down, facing her. "I told you seven-thirty"

"Fashionably late"

"You shouldn't keep a girl waiting"

"You shouldn't have picked such a busy location"

A moment captured the tension as eye contact locked.

"Would you like a drink?" Tina asked.

"Sure. What are you drinking?"

Tina stirred her cocktail. "Tequila sunrise. But you can have whatever you want."

"Oh I can, can I....."

Tina moved her satin scarf and lifted her leather handbag from the back of her chair.

"No, I'll get it" said Mike, slipping his hand into his wallet pocket.

"Michael. I insist...."

She had complete power over him, but he couldn't let her show it off.

"Okay. Then I'll go for a mojito."

Tina slipped her bag over her slender shoulder and walked towards the bar. Mike's eyes followed her steps, as a huntsman silently observes a deer. The barman who served Tina was a good looking man with large biceps. The man was pleased to serve such a beautiful woman but their conversation was far out of earshot. To avoid feelings of jealousy Mike looked at his phone. He had a message and a missed call. The message was from his bank, indicating the successful arrival of the one thousand three hundred and ninety-six pounds. The missed call was from Richie, who

had gone so far as to leave a voicemail. The voice was downtrodden. "Hi Uncle Mike, nice of you to call. Yeah Mum told me about your bet. Burger sounds good."
"You look worried" observed Tina, who was back with his drink. It occurred to Mike that he had not told Tina anything about his private life. Before he had time to respond, Tina stopped him.
"Don't be. Tonight you have nothing to worry about."
'She's so playful' he thought.
"Right" he said, "so what's all this about?"
"All what?"
"These drinks, this location"
"Well, like I wrote you, I enjoyed your company at Dawn's party, but there were a lot of people to focus attention on"
"So now you're meeting each guest, on a one-to-one basis?"
"Not every guest....... just a few."
She continued to stir her drink, moving her eyes away from his. Mike noticed her thin, rose-gold necklace with an arrow pendant. It hung so delicately around her neck. Her pendant earrings also caught his eyes as they dangled just below her lobes. Tina was mesmeric and Mike wondered how this situation had ever come to fruition. The sun had set outside, leaving the sky a dark purple blue.
"It looks like Kevin had fun on Friday!"
"Ha! Yeah, he let himself loose. His outfit was so funny"
"Oh, my god. Tell me about it! He makes the perfect Gimli"
"Jack was very accommodating. He's a really cool guy"
"Yeah. Jack's great. He's a proper movie buff and he's into, shall we say, stylish things"
"Are you and him close?"
"Uhm, I'd say he's closer to Dawn than me. But yeah, in terms of cousin's we're close. Anyway, he's been talking about you and Kevin all weekend. Or so Dawn tells me"

Mike made a silent prayer Tina wouldn't ask him about his family.
"By the way" he said, "who were those *Avatar* girls?"
"Oh, they are some of Dawn's friends. She met them at this vegan cooking class"
Mike nodded and took a gulp from his drink. The crushed ice touched his lips as the mint, lime and rum slid down his trachea.
"Well, you got one thing right" said Tina. She was always doing this Mike thought. Raising mystery.
"What?"
"You came smart" she said, eyeing him up and down. A full body scan.
"Thanks. I mean, you don't look bad yourself"
They both took sips from their drinks and then in a moment of complete chance said the same thing, as if their brains had synchronised.
"Guess what?"
"Guess what?"
Tina found it hilarious but insisted that Mike went first, tapping her finger rings on the table.
"I won over a thousand pounds"
"What!? Seriously?"
"Seriously"
"How?"
"I put a bet on the football. An accumulator"
"That's craaaaaazy" she replied, her American accent making him laugh.
"So you're a gambling man?"
"I believe in taking risks" he said, "now your turn"
"I'll tell you upstairs"
"Upstairs?"
"Yeah, I've booked us a room."

Tina led Mike mysteriously to her aforementioned room. Through sliding glass doors, down marble corridors. She led the way because she could. She knew the way.
"Where are you taking me?"
"You'll see" she teased, curving her neck to giggle at him. Mike felt his downstairs stiffen against his chinos, so while she wasn't looking he did a quick rearrange.
'I can't let her see my bulge.'
Tina's heels tapped up a short corner flight of stairs and Mike took another look at his phone to avoid those sensations of over-eagerness.
"Here we are" Tina stated, removing a slim black keycard from her purse. She slid it slowly into the slot and heard the click. Mike was caught in the trance of that beauty spot on her cheek.
"Wait until you see this."
The door opened up to an impeccably clean and spacious room. The floor was designed with silvery grey marble. A large king size with black fitted sheets, a clouded white duvet and long stretched pillows sat silently beneath an incredible, large glass chandelier.
Tina kicked off her shoes, using her big toe and second toe to slip off the heel of the second one.
"Look at that ceiling!"
Mike did as he was told and looked directly up. He saw himself staring up back down at him. It felt like that paradigm where it's hard to tell if the staircase is going upwards or downwards. The entire ceiling was a glass mirror, optically expanding the size of the hotel room.
"Time to tell me about your "guess what" or, he paused, looking back at her, "is this it?"
"No" said Tina, in that tone women use to tease men, "your guess what is right here." She unzipped a small black

suitcase which had been waiting in the room, then removed Mike's silver hip flask, wiping down the top with a Kleenex.
"I filled it with rum."
Mike quickly unscrewed the cap. "Cheers" he said before taking a gulp. His Adam's apple bobbed like a buoy out at sea.
"Want some?" he offered Tina.
"Sure"
He threw the bottle gently back at her.
"Nice under-arm" she said upon catching it.
Mike walked around the bed, observing more of this strange room. Three of the walls were cushion-padded, all jet black. The fourth wall was pure window, looking out over a skylit city. It was raining, just like it always did in this place, but right then in that moment did Mike feel that warming sensation of being on the inside looking out. Raindrops hammered against the pains of glass, then slid downwards in a blurred game of Tetris.
"This must have cost a fortune" he said, letting go of all tension and falling backwards onto the bed.
"Don't worry. You can subsidise me with your gambling money"
"I could" said Mike.
"Oh" expressed Tina, steering the conversation, "I requested two things with the room. No TV and smoking permitted. I figured between us we would be way too entertained to watch a movie."
Tina stood up from her cross-legged position against the wall, and walked ever so slowly towards Mike.
"The other night was just fiction" she stated, opening a fresh packet of Camel cigarettes, "tonight is real life."

Tina prowled onto the bed. A lioness pawing at her curled hair. She crawled up Mike's legs, slowly sliding her right palm up the inside seam of his trousers. As she arched her back up towards his face and then pulled away, he caught the smell of spiced vanilla parfúm.

"Take off my dress" she whispered. Mike could feel his penis pulsating as Tina lifted her arms to allow him. He sat up, reached an arm around and began to slowly slide her silver zip. As he did so she kissed his neck with her lips. Mike grabbed her dress by the hips and lifted, revealing a tight caramel stomach and a dainty space-grey bra.

"Oh my god" he said before she stopped him by putting a finger on his lips.

"Stop. I'm tired of guys compliments. I actually find them a massive turn-off. The reason I like you is because, well, you're normal."

"Normal?"

She laughed, "Just shut up Michael".

Tina moved her hands towards his crotch and undid his button. Mike was stuck in a moment of limbo, caught directly between heaven and hell.

'Is she an angel or a devil?' he thought.

As she undid the fly and began pulling his trousers down, he blurted out a nervous comment.

"It's Sunday night."

Tina continued to pull them down.

"Worry about that later" she said, ignoring the vibration inside his trouser pocket. Her hips and breasts were so curvaceous, her beauty spot so perfect. Her arrow necklace pierced his heart, injecting it with lust demons. She sat away from him and rubbed his manhood through his boxer shorts, forcing it to excrete some pre-cum.

"Oh I almost forgot! I have champagne chilling in the fridge."

Tina swept the duvet clean of removed clothes, jumped off the bed and went to the refrigerator.

"Have you ever wished you could just forget real life and lose yourself in a night of pure passion?"

"I have" he said. "Many times."

She popped the cork and drank straight from the bottle. Mike pictured her body sweating like the condensation that surrounded the ice cold champagne bottle.

"Open your mouth" she demanded, before pouring the champagne into it, biting his neck a little.

Mike's phone was vibrating again.

"Sometimes you can trust in someone better" she said softly, reaching her fingertips underneath the elastic band of his briefs. "When you don't know anything about them" he finished.

"Do you trust me?" she asked, revealing his prized possession.

"I trust you" he said, rolling back his eyes into his skull.

Chapter 34

The post-orgasm tranquility, that dreamlike trance of pure bliss, was interrupted by another phone vibration.
"I've got to answer that"
"If you say so" she said, kissing his dried lips.
Mike, completely naked, scrambled into the pocket of his scrunched up chinos and hit green.
"Hello?"
"Mike, seriously where the fuck are you? I tried phoning you like five times tonight!"
Mike thought of his mother.
"Uhm," he said standing up, desperate to buy time. "I had to help out a friend after leaving Chris'"
"Well it's half-past midnight and I need your help. It's an emergency Mike. Toby is coughing up blood." Sharon had serious panic in her voice, "I'm terrified Mike, I don't know what to do!"
"I've got to go" he mouthed to Tina,
"Where? Why?"
"I'll tell you tomorrow, I'm sorry" he said, and then he left the room.

There was trouble in paradise. A devil in heaven, an angel in hell. His thoughts flickered between the recent past and the near future. Never in his life had he imaged a scenario like the one he had just had with Tina. But he had been cursed for divulging with foreign forbidden fruit. God's timing could not have been more bittersweet, as Toby had finally chosen his day to do something dramatic. Sharon sounded extremely preoccupied on the phone, and now Mike felt the guilt. At that moment he didn't regret what had happened with Tina, he couldn't feel regret for something he had enjoyed so much, but that pang of guilt

struck his heart like a lightning bolt. He pushed open the heavy glass door of the hotel and went out into the rain. He didn't know what to think. Cars had vacated the hotel, so it was easier for Mike to find his vehicle than it had been to park it earlier. His denim shirt didn't take long to soak through, and once he opened his car door and sat down in the seat, he lit up a cigarette and wound the window down a touch to allow some breathability. A text message came through from Sharon, explaining that she had arrived at the emergency vets with Toby. She left an address and told Mike to come right away. It wasn't what he was expecting, and the panic grew inside him like a thorned rose. Pricking his insides so that it was impossible to get comfortable. His cigarette burned quickly, and the ash fell onto his lap, marking his chinos.
"Fuck" he said, wiping the ash into the material.
He threw the butt out of the window, and sent a quick reply to Sharon.

On my way x

Mike twisted the key and held down the clutch, starting the car engine. He pulled out of his space, and followed the exit signs to get back out onto the city streets. He was drunk, and could feel the alcohol disrupting his central nervous system. He hoped that he wouldn't get stopped by the police, and at the first set of traffic lights he thought of an excuse to Sharon as to why he was drunk on a Sunday night.
'I had a few drinks with my football mates to celebrate my winnings'. It was that simple.
A car horn beeped him at the lights, which had changed from red to green without Mike realising. He over-revved

the engine and continued on his way to the vets, trying hard not to panic. He didn't really know where he was going, so he had to put the directions into the GPS on his smart phone. He felt distracted, lost, confused, agitated. Just as he was finishing off inputting the irritably long address, another text message came through.

I can't believe you left without giving me a reason. Safe to say you killed the vibe. I'll see you in work tomorrow I guess...

He swiped the message away, and confirmed the address on his phone. Green lines highlighted his route, and an annoying female robot spoke to him through the phone speaker.
"Continue half a mile down Glendon Street, then take the last exit at the roundabout."
Tina was upset. Sharon was upset. Mike was intoxicated, suffocating from his own sins. Taxi's jumped in front of him, switching lanes consistently. Mike thought he had to delete that message on his phone, just in case Sharon needed to use his mobile for whatever reason. He had to cover his tracks, now that he was derailing.

The rain harshened, forcing the necessity for windscreen wipers. The night blurred past him, lights distracting him.

Where are you Mike? Hurry I think he's going to die!

Mike put his foot down and leaned forward to try and see through the heavy water droplets which had become to accumulate on his window. The wipers were on full speed, battering against the oncoming downpour.

"Take the next right onto Weldon Road"
He did a right, ignoring the indicator, which he didn't think about until he caught sight of them. That familiar red and blue flash. Mike cracked his neck from side to side and eased off the accelerator pedal. He was just a couple of minutes away, but was in a state of panic as a police vehicle drove around the corner, right by him. Mike held his breath, and thankfully they didn't stop. No, that wasn't the way his night was going to end. Not locked up behind bars inebriated.

Chapter 35

Once he'd finally arrived he parked his car right behind Sharon's, pressed up against the pavement. The emergency vets wasn't a big place, but there were a couple of people inside the orange tinted room. Mike could see them through the window of his car. He could see the back of Sharon's head, and a sickly Toby drooped over her shoulder, eyes closed. He slipped a cigarette out of his box, and sparked it up inside the car. The rain continued and he didn't want to mess around trying to light it outside. He took two or three strong pulls on it, pulled his car keys out of the ignition, and got out the car.

A door bell made a ring as he entered the vets, stinking of the cigarette smoke and looking like a drowned fish. Sharon was at the front of the line now, being seen to. She looked over her shoulder and saw Mike, then turned back to the lady who was attending to her.

"It's my dog, I don't know what to do. There's blood."

Mike sifted past an old couple who were also with a dog, and moved towards Sharon to give her some support.

"Hey, what's going on?"

Sharon responded coldly, immediately icing him out of the situation. "I'm sorting it Mike"

"Yeah?" he responded, taken aback.

"Yes, I said I'm sorting it. Go and wait in the car."

Mike said, "I'll wait over here", which Sharon didn't seem to like, but she turned back round to the receptionist who had called for a vet to come and collect Toby immediately. Mike sat down next to a guy who had his eyes closed. It was clear this man had been waiting for some time for his favourite pet to return from surgery.

The kind receptionist continued, “Obviously… sorry what's his name?"
"Sorry?"
"Your dog"
"Oh, Toby"
The receptionist smiled and nodded gently.
"Obviously Toby requires immediate attention, just like most of the animals that get brought here at this time on a Sunday night. We will do everything we can to help Toby but of course, you have to understand that we require payment immediately due to the method of service.
"Of course," Sharon said, "can I pay on card?"
"Of course madam"
"Do you need to use my card?" Mike asked, rather loudly.
"No, I don't Mike. I said to wait in the car. I'm handling it.”
The old couple turned to each other, the receptionist concentrated on entering her customer's card into the card-reader, but the seated man still had his eyes closed.
"What's your problem?" Mike blurted out. The alcohol, stress and adrenaline taking control over him. The room fell silent, except for a few beeping noises which could be heard from behind the receptionist's counter. Sharon ignored him, sensing a rise in temperature.
"Seriously, Shaz, what's your problem? I'm here aren't I?"
"Not now Mike" she demanded.
A thin, tall man with spectacles arrived to take Toby into the operating theatre in the back. Sharon popped her four digit pin into the card reader, and then the receptionist told her that she would have to wait.
"No problem" she replied, "any idea how long the wait will be?"
"I'm sorry, every case is unique. We'll let you know as soon as we know something madam."

Sharon thanked the lady, then turned around and head towards the exit.
"Where are you going?" asked Mike, who was growing increasingly impatient with his wife. The sleeping man opened his eyes to decipher the situation.
"Outside" said Sharon, opening the door and letting it close behind her.

Mike followed his wife out of the vets. She had gone and got into her car to avoid the rain. Mike attempted to open the passenger side door but it was locked from the inside.
"Shaz, what the fuck is going on?"
"You don't know?"
Mike thought.
"No, I don't."
"Do you think I'm stupid Mike?" she said, staring at him outside getting soaked in the downpour.
"No," he repeated, "I don't"
The click of the door unlocking surprised him. He clambered into his wife's car.
"Please" he said, wiping his face from the rain drops, "can you please tell me what's the matter!"
She stared at him. Her eyes vacant with lost hope.
"What have I done!?" he demanded in a raised voice.
"Where shall I start Mike? Oh yeah, let's start with the lie that you told me. Maybe then we can unravel a few more of your lies." Her tone was as hard and cold as a rockface.
"Lie?" he replied, acting all puzzled.
"Yes Mike. I phoned Chris. You never went to his house to drop off the PlayStation did you?"
He tried to respond, but she cut him off immediately.
"Don't. You're only going to make it worse. In fact, I bet that stupid thing is sitting in the boot of your car right now

isn't it. Tell me I'm wrong," she said, and then again louder, "TELL ME I'M WRONG!" Blood rushed to her face.
The colour drained from Mike's. He had never seen her like this before.
"What's more Mike, is you finally turn up to come and help me and Toby. After me phoning your mobile like five times. And" she stammered, "and, you *stink* of alcohol. Drink-driving hey? What a great idea that is!" She let out a pretend laugh, some type of exasperated guffaw. "But that's not all Mike, you smell of other things too."
"What?"
"Oh, I don't know. How about a sweet scented female perfume. Vanilla is it? What, you didn't think I could notice it through all the stale smell of cigarettes?"
"Vanilla?" said Mike, his face remaining rigid, his internal organs trying their hardest to squirm his way out of it.
"Which leads me all to one conclusion Mike. You smell of guilt."
She grabbed his hand, to reveal the red mark caused by Tina's whip.
"I saw this the other day, and for whatever reason I didn't think to ask you about it. I don't know, maybe I was too caught up in my sister's marital problems. I have no idea what caused this but I find it, shall we say, out of the ordinary. Care to explain?"
"Well, on Friday when I was with the lads, we were playing pool and a ball bounced off the table and hit my hand."
His phone buzzed in his pocket.
"Likely story Mike," said his wife, hearing his phone vibration, "what's that? You should probably answer that, no?"
His face distorted into a crippled culpability, like a stage actor who had forgotten his lines.

"Get out of my car Mike"
"What? Why?"
"Because," she said, lighting up a menthol to calm herself down. "Because you're a bullshitter. I don't trust you anymore. I don't know where you've been tonight and I don't think I want to know the truth."
"But-"
"But nothing. I'm going to move in with Steph for a while. She's going through a rough time. Me too. Family first, you know?" she said, twisting the proverbial knife into his gut. "Remember one thing Mike, liars always get found out...."
There was no getting through to her now. Mike knew they would have to talk another time. So he turned to get out of the car and just as he did; his mobile slipped out of his pocket. That's when Sharon saw it. Her name at the top of the message. Tina.
"You're disgusting" she said, and as hard as she could, she slapped him across the face with a stern hand.

Escape

So, did you enjoy your holiday Doc?

Michael, it's so nice to see you again. Yes, I did thank you. Thanks for asking. But we aren't here to talk about me, are we? No, no, tell me what's going on with you.

Well, I hate to come across as, shall we say, overdramatic, but it's somewhat of a miracle that I'm even here.

What? How so?

I woke up on Sunday with a corn sack pulled over my face. A gag in my mouth, pulled tight so my saliva soaked through the rope. I remember being curled up inside a vehicle, probably in the trunk because of my position and the smell of the car exhaust. I tried to make noises but the driver had the car stereo on. There was nothing I could do.

Michael. Are you safe?

I don't think anyone is safe Doc. Not from the pitfalls of life. Anyway, there was no conveniently placed blade to cut myself free. My hands were tied just as tight as my gag and my ankles were tied together too. I literally had no idea what was going on. All I can remember from that journey, was relaxing my muscles and falling into a state of unconsciousness. The next time I awoke, and I kid you not, I was fucking hanging upside down inside some kind of fish factory. Typical triad money launder cover up. So, this asian fella ripped the corn sack off my head and started shouting in my face. Spitting all over me he was. Of course,

I couldn't understand a word he was saying, and I couldn't tell him that because of my mouth gag.

Hanging upside down? What do you mean?

I mean that I was suspended from some fish hook by my legs, with all the blood rushing to my head. Plus I'm sure I'd been anaesthetised because my body felt all woozy and jelly-like, and my mind wasn't fully registering things. Anyway, I nodded my head backwards as if to beckon the Chinese guy, and luckily he walked towards me to remove my gag. Back in the penitentiary a coupla guys had taught me a few tricks to get out of trouble, and this was one of those moments when you rely on special skills like that. As he removed the rope from my mouth, I lifted my tied wrists over the back of his head and pulled sharp and tight, breaking the guys neck. As he fell back, the weight of his body stretched the rope I was hanging from, which began to sever on the meat hook. I fell on top of his body, searched his corpse and found a short blade to help cut myself loose.

Are you actually “for real” here Michael?

Oh you better believe it Doc. Whilst you were topping up your tan and sipping your fourth Sex on the Beach, I was alone, cold, drugged and hunted inside a cartel hideout. Finally free from all ties, I realised I had no gun and no mobile phone. I thought of my wife and kids, like most men do when they are in the face of danger. A man is a man until he needs the love and support of his family right?

Right

So, I took this short blade and held it tight in my palm with the blade facing down. I could hear more men heading towards the area, shouting fierce Mandarin to one another. I kept low, and head towards the shadows in the corner. I knew I needed to escape, but I also knew this would come at a price. I needed to kill more men. I needed to fight my way to freedom.

I have to say, I am not sure therapy is your best option right now Michael. Should you not be looking at some kind of witness protection program? From what you told me in our last session, and what you are telling me now. It sounds like you are public enemy number one for the gangs that reside in this city.

Just shut up and listen would ya? So I crept amongst the boxes, crates and forklift trucks. The place stunk of raw fish and sweat. I heard footsteps running towards the scene of the crime, and through a gap in the crates I could see the AK47 rifles that the men carried. They must have been telling each other to spread out and search for me, because that's exactly what they did. I kept low and I kept silent. The men dispersed and kept turning around pointing their guns in all directions. I could hear one of them approaching me, and caught a glance of a pistol holstered inside a leather belt around his waist. I knew this was my chance, so as he sidestepped around the forklift truck I grabbed him fiercely round the neck and wrapped my hand over his mouth to shush him. Choking him out, I grabbed his pistol, shimmied out of my hiding place and shot down the other three guys. It's all about outsmarting your enemy, you see.

Sounds very, well, "professional".

Uhuh. It kinda was Doc.

Did you make it out then?

I'm sitting here aren't I?

You are. Well, unfortunately that's time Michael. We'll have a look at dissecting this situation next time. Make the payment to the usual account, and of course, please try and stay safe.

Chapter 36

Sharon and Steph were sitting on the sofa at Steph's house. They were the only two in the house, free from the enclosed broodiness of male figures.

"I just can't believe it" said Steph. "I mean I know how Tony can be. Hell, *you* know how Tony can be. But I never expected him to cheat on me." A couple of tears began to roll down her soft cheeks. Sharon consoled her by holding her hand.

"How many emails were there?" asked Sharon, who had still not informed Steph about what had happened with Mike.

"About fifty Sha!" More tears followed. Sniffles too. "I just can't believe it" she stuttered, on the edge of an emotional breakdown.

Sharon was trying her hardest to retain control of herself, at least for her sister's sake. She knew her sister better than anyone, and felt like today was a perfect moment for them both to let everything out.

"And what did they say?" she asked, "I mean, if you don't mind me asking."

Steph made those helpless weeping noises. Half hiccuping half choking.

"Ho-" she began to reply, until Sharon passed her a tissue to blow her nose and wipe her eyes.

"Horrible things" she finally mustered the power to say. "Flirting and talking about sex and stuff. The things that he wanted to do to her"

"Seriously? What a pig. I can't believe it." said Sharon. "So, what, all this supposed time gambling? That was him going..."

"Yes"

"I'm so sorry Steph."
They looked at each other in the eyes. Steph's flooded in liquid, Sharon's welling up. The silence of the room accompanied them both, moisturising the intensity of their conversation. The TV was off, the curtains drawn together, and a soft white candle burned on the mantelpiece.
"How has Richie handled the situation?" asked Sharon, wiping away a tear of her own. Steph took a fresh tissue from the packet and blew her nose loudly. Clearing her sinuses from congealed snots.
"Like he always does. He goes silent and enclosed. He's always been introverted, and this shit clearly doesn't help."
Sharon looked at her sister with pity. She looked so beautiful, even right now upset and full of cold. Sharon had always been jealous of her sister's good looks, but they had always got on well. Growing up, Sharon always wondered why Steph had it all. The boyfriends in High School, the special parental attention, the bigger bedroom. Their mother had always favoured Stephanie, but their father had a special bond with Sharon. "Don't be jealous of your sister" he would always say to her, "You are the most considerate person in this family, and that's a special quality!" Just thinking about her father triggered her to shed more tears, so now both the sisters were crying.
Steph continued, "I don't even know where Richie is right now. I doubt he's still going to college. Not with all this that's going on."
"Maybe he is, maybe studying is keeping him occupied. He's always been academic"
"I guess"
"Don't worry about him, he'll be fine Steph."
Steph started to sob. Physically breaking down on the sofa until her body curled up into the foetal position.

"My biggest fear is that he ends up like his father."
Sharon nodded in agreement.
"Tony has always been hard on him, which hasn't helped with Rich's personality. That's why it always felt like a breath of fresh air having you and Mike over. Richie loves Mike."
Sharon wiped her eyes. Just hearing his name made her angry. It wasn't fair of her to keep it any longer from her sister. She got up off the sofa and head towards the stairs.
"I'll be back in a minute" said Sharon, bawling her eyes out as she climbed the staircase.

Sharon slumped herself on the toilet seat, knickers pulled down by her ankles, head distraught in hands. She cried and cried and thought. She was so bitterly disappointed about what she had discovered with her own husband. She saw it coming with Tony, but never with Mike. She loved him, and couldn't understand why he had never fully reciprocated that love. She tried to come to terms as to why he had done whatever he had done. She didn't deserve being lied to, and she didn't think that he deserved her love and care anymore. Mike had been sending her messages all morning, begging her to "come home and talk" about it, but she didn't want to. It was that simple.
"Shaaaa?" Steph shouted up the stairs.
Sharon was unaware of how long she had been gone, and quickly tried to pull herself together. She wiped her tears with the back of her hand, and hadn't applied any make-up that morning that could be smudged.
"Coming" she replied, in a wobbly voice that Steph recognised to be out of the ordinary. Sharon pulled up her knickers and walked over to the sink to splash her face with water to disguise her tears. Her face in the bathroom mirror

was a perfect reflection of her current state. A devastated woman filled with undeserved pain. As she unlocked the bathroom door and opened it, there stood her sister.
"Oh sis, what on earth's the matter?" cried Steph, opening her arms for Sharon to fall into. This was enough to set Sharon off again, as the two sisters locked into each other and wept in waves.

Once they had eventually sat back downstairs and put the kettle on, Sharon proceeded to tell Steph her tale of woe. It was a conversation loaded with honesty and softness, far from the deceit of man.
"So it all started when, well, I don't actually know when it started, but I had my suspicions on Friday when he told me he was going to have a weekend with the boys."
"What started? Are you talking about Mike"
"Exactly. Let's put it this way, I don't think you are the only one whose husband is having an affair."
Steph's jaw dropped, revealing an open hole of consternation.
"What? What do you mean Sha'? What? You mean? Mike's doing the same as Tony?" she said, broken puzzled.
"I don't know if it's quite the same, but like I said I found it strange when he told me he was going to see his football friends. I mean, he hasn't spent time with them in years and years. I guess that he could have been catching up with them, but I couldn't help but feel like there was something fishy about his story."
Steph rubbed Sharon's shoulder to try and comfort her. Both sets of eyes were red, puffy, swelled up.
"And?"
"Well, I contacted him a couple of times that night, but to no avail. Not on Friday night nor Saturday morning. Anyway, then we had the meal at the Chinese restaurant. I

know the attention was on Tony and his behaviour, because you had told me to pay attention to him, but I also couldn't help but feel like Mike was hiding something. Of course, once he revealed the news about the money he had won, I figured that was the thing he had been so snoopy about."
She got further upset.
"Okay. Yeah, I mean like you said I was too busy worrying about Ton'"
"Well, Mike woke up kinda strangely Sunday morning. Saying he had a headache and such. A bad dream or something."
"A bad dream? About what?"
"This is the thing. He said it was about Richie."
Steph was taken aback slightly. Her face utter confusion.
"Our Rich?"
"Apparently. Anyway, I popped out to the shops to get a few bits and bobs in and then when I got back, that's when the whole Toby incident happened."
"And where was Mike?"
Sharon stopped. Her head bowed and tears fell into her dirty blonde hair.
"Oh, honey I'm so so sorry" said Steph, and the sisters felt pain.
Sharon went on to recount the rest of the story, and then asked if it was okay if she moved in for a while. The candle flickered so softly on the mantelpiece. The black mirror of the television was off, no music played, no food was cooking. The room and the air were still and chilling, heated only by the warmth of the love these two broken hearted sisters shared for each other. They were family, and they had each other. No matter what.

Chapter 37

His heart was pulsating. His respiratory system inhaling exhaling like mad. His feet kept moving and moving and moving and his arms were in perfect unison like a well oiled machine. It was dark out, that black sky spread over his city, heavy as lead. Stomp stomp went his feet, the rucksack adjustable straps pulled tightly in front of him. The contents of which were a pencil, a novel, a notepad, a bottle of water, a large bag of crisps and a white rubber. His trainers splashed in the shallow puddles that filled every crevice of the backroad, down by the passage that lead to the train station. A rabbit darted in front of him so quickly it knocked him off balance. He stopped, and with his eyes followed its path into the shadows. His arms automatically fell to his laps, and he panted like the fox which lurked these surroundings. He rubbed his eye aggressively, then spotted his shoelaces had come loose. As he bent down to tie them back up, his mobile phone buzzed in his jeans pocket.

Where the hell are you? We are worried sick. Call us xxx

"We?" he questioned. "Us?"
He looked at his wrist watch, it read 21:43. He only had four minutes to get there. So he unzipped his back pack, threw his phone in there, zipped it back up and put it back on his back.
'No time for replies right now' he thought.

His legs were getting so heavy now, and the lights began to appear in the distance. The steady sounding chug of the wheels rotating on the iron tracks dated back long before this moment. Richie kept sprinting as fast as he

could until he could see a man in a yellow vest right outside the ticket gate. Just to the right of the barrier. He kept his legs moving though, devising a plan whilst the train was edging closer and closer to the platform. Richie didn't have time to pay for a ticket, in fact, he didn't even have his wallet with him. He must have forgotten it. Back in his room with the torn down posters. He had no choice other than to jump the gate and ignore the yellow-vested man.
"Hey son where are you going" the man questioned, as he saw Richie's refusal to slow down his speed. "Can I help?" Richie ignored him and continued on his path.
"Excuse me sir, do you have your ticket?" asked the man, more formally this time. Richie timed his momentum and as he approached the gate, swung his right leg up with his knee bent, so that he could catch the rim of the circular barrier and hoist his way over it. The yellow-vested man reached out to grab him, but only managed to clutch the shoulder of Richie's hoody.
"You can't board the train without a ticket young man." Richie wrestled his way out of the man's grip, and scuffled his way over. The train hissed and came to a standstill. Richie continued moving, not realising that the train which had approached was on the opposite platform. He had come too far now. Too far not to catch the first train he could see. So he grabbed tight on his backpack straps, and hot footed up the stairwell which acted as a tunnel between platform 1 and platform 2. He could hear the security guy following him, and knew that there were probably cameras tracking his manoeuvres. Yet his legs would slow down for no-one. They made their way up the stairs as Richie grabbed onto the corner of the wall to allow himself to swing round and keep moving. It would be any moment now before the train continued on its designated route; all he had to do was keep

moving and make his way down the stairwell on the other side. His mind made the involuntary decision to tackle two steps at a time, which was fortunate, because the doors were closing as Richie managed to slip through them just in time.

He locked himself in the toilet cubicle, and sat on top of the toilet lid. Gasping for fresh air yet receiving oxygen laced with stale urine and wet stool. The smell of the urinal was atrocious, but once again he had no choice. It was stay here and hide, or face the consequences of hitching a free ride on a high speed train. He unzipped his bag, consumed the majority of his bottle of water, and then reached for his phone. He had no intention of replying to his mother, but felt like he owed at least someone an explanation. So he started to type a new message.

Dear Uncle Mike. I am leaving town. I'm a young adult now and there is nothing but disappointment here. Mum and Dad are splitting up, as she has now uncovered the truth about him sleeping around with other women. Honestly, I don't want to be caught in the middle of this shit. It's taken me some time to realise, but I'm better off on my own. I know I told you I would be up for getting that burger with you, but it will have to be another time. I'm telling you because you understand. Dad is a piece of shit. He's never been a real father to me, and now he's disappointed Mum as well. I'm on a train to nowhere. Don't worry about me, I'll be in touch. Rich

Chapter 38

Tina got up extra early that morning. The hotel room which had once seemed comfortable, now felt like a place of shame and secrecy. She couldn't lie in that bed alone, thinking about how the night might have gone differently. She couldn't understand what it was about British guys, with their refusal to say things as they really are. She just wasn't able to figure out what had happened, and she wasn't going to spend any more time trying to justify things in her head. The bathroom was her safe haven, and so she climbed out of the bed, sleepy eyed, and unzipped her compact, black suitcase. The silver zippers slid so smoothly, allowing her to open up the case and find her make-up and toiletries bag. She removed it from the case and walked over to the bathroom, which to her surprise, contained one of those neat little coffee machines which had become so popular as of late. A capsule stand was erect next to the machine, so she chose a pale blue capsule, filled the machine water tank, and pressed the button. As the machine made a grinding noise, and the hot water combined with the coffee, Tina removed her clothes and slid open the crystal shower door. Feeling the temperature with her toes, she waited until the ice cold got warmer. She allowed the fresh hot water to hit her directly in the face, and enjoyed the sensation of the water running over her scalp, through her hair. Her eyelids were closed, but with tension. She kept her eyes closed, but loosened the tightness of her temples. She felt that release as the black of her vision changed shade due to the light of the bathroom. She squeezed some white shower gel into her soft hands, and rubbed it over her stomach and bosoms. Mike still hadn't replied to her messages, and she wondered if things would be awkward in the office. That reminded her, she needed to brush her teeth thoroughly, so as to disguise the smell of alcohol which evidently lingered on her breath.

She checked out of the hotel early, and bought an overpriced croissant to eat in the car. A Stevie Nicks song was coming to an end on the radio, and as the hour struck eight o'clock, she was greeted by the news. It was still dark outside, as is customary in the winter months, but it wasn't raining. A celebrity had passed away during the night, some actor from the seventies, of whom she knew nothing about. There had been another mass shooting in the USA, in which seventeen college students had lost their lives. Details weren't clear other than the assailant was still on the loose, and the President was due to speak later in the day about clamping down on their beloved firearm amendment. Tina shook her head in shock, wondering how her family back in Philadelphia were dealing with the news. The fatal attack had taken place in Washington DC not too far from her hometown, and so she made a mental note to call her mom on her work break.

"And finally, an accident between two vehicles occurred last night not far from the city centre. A man, now inside police custody, was speeding down the motorway and swerved his vehicle suddenly as it appeared to be drifting into oncoming traffic. The driver, who police currently want to remain anonymous, hit another car in the lane to his right, causing the accident that has left a family of three deceased. Among the victims were Mr and Mrs Goodwin, and their infant daughter who was just three years old. It is thought that the driver was under the influence of alcohol. More to come on this story later." Tina turned the radio off, preferring the silence of the morning drive to the consistent terrible news.

The car park was quiet once she arrived, and there was no sign of Mike's car.
'He's never on time to work anyway' she thought, heading through the front door and over to the lift. As the doors closed she was alone, and so she straightened her work attire and moved her face closer to the mirror for inspection. She breathed a single breath into the palm of her hand, and proceeded to smell her hand as a means to checking. Her lipstick was perfect, her hair too, hence one of the reasons why she got up so early. As the lift doors opened to the office, only Kevin was at his computer.
"Morning Kevin" she smiled, wondering how much he knew. How close him and Mike really were.
"Morning Tina, thanks for the other"
Tina pressed an index finger to her lips. Reminding Kevin that no-one else in the office knew about the fancy dress party.
"It's okay" she said.
"Sorry" he replied silently.
"You're here early aren't you?" she asked, making small talk.
"Yeah, I wanted to start the week on a positive note" he said, "and I've got a mountain of emails to reply to."
"You and me both" she said, sitting at her desk. She switched on her computer and while it loaded up, she nipped into the kitchen to make a green tea.
"The kettle's boiling Kevin, would you like a drink?"
"Nah I've got a brew already" he said, "thanks though." He continued working, and considered asking Tina at some point today how Dawn was doing. He hadn't realised it at the time, but he had taken quite a shine to Dawn, as well as one of the *Avatar* girls.
"Okay" said Tina, watching the kettle take forever to boil.

As she carried her hot drink back to her desk, the lift doors sprung open to reveal Carol, Barbara and Ian. Ian was midway through some anecdote when he turned and saw Tina at her desk.
“And how is the most beautiful colleague I ever had doing?” he asked, walking over to his desk.
“I don’t know, I haven’t spoken to Carol all weekend” she replied nonchalantly.
“Ha!” went Ian, “That’s a good one”
“Hmph” was the only noise Tina made, wondering how she was going to manage another week next to this creep.
“But seriously,” he continued, leaning on her side of the double desk, “good weekend?”
“Eventful”
“Really? How come?” he continued to pry.
“Just joking. Another weekend watching TV sitcoms.”
“Ahh you’re always joking aren’t you. What you watching?”
Tina continued to reply with short answers, and wished she could put her earphones in and just ignore Ian. Barbara and Carol were at it again, jabbering away about who had been voted off this week’s episode of reality TV, and who was the most handsome judge. They were harmless, thought Tina, but just so loud.
“Oh Babs, I’m not I’m fussed about it anymore. I mean, now they’ve voted off Steve. There’s no eye candy is there!”
“What are ya like Caz? You know he just had to go this week. That’s three weeks in a row now he’s been in the bottom two!”
“That’s true” she said, turning round. “Morning Kevin, morning Tina.”

At twenty five past nine, Mr Hardy arrived. Suited up as always, running his active fingers down his skinny tie. He must have sprayed a tonne of aftershave, because Tina could smell him a mile off. It was that one that came in a blue bottle, the shape of a buff man's torso.
'How original' she thought.
"Morning Mr Hardy" said Babs, smiling obtrusively.
"Morning Mr Hardy" copied Carol.
"Good morning ladies" he said, walking straight past them and into his office.
Mike was nowhere to be seen, and Tina began to wonder what the hell was going on. On the one hand she didn't give a shit, but on the other hand she felt a little responsible. She had received no emails from him, something she thought might have been a possibility, and so she decided to send him one final sms. Just as she was doing so, an email came through to her inbox. It was from Hardy.

Morning Tina,
Would you come and speak to me in my office please. When you have a spare moment of course.

'How odd' she thought. Wondering why he hadn't just told her in person. She hated the ways bosses utilised their power in such trivial ways. It was either that or that British pride again. She knocked back the rest of her green tea and headed straight towards his office door.
"Where are you going?" asked Ian. Tina turned and looked confused.
"To, see Hardy..." she turned back and continued towards his large door. She tapped slightly and the blind opened

from the inside so she could see into his office. Hardy beckoned her in.
"Hey Tina, how are you doing? Take a seat, please." Hardy shuffled around a little, rearranging a few things on his desk, such as a paperweight and a photo of his family.
"Morning, did you have a nice weekend?" she asked, thinking if she brought up the weekend first, he perhaps wouldn't go into finding out too much about hers.
"Yeah, you know" he smiled, cracking his fingers, "Family time. And you?"
"Uhm, nothing much. I just spent some time with my cousin, watching movies and stuff."
Mr Hardy smiled so genuinely and looked directly at Tina. Her American accent melted his mouth into a dimpled curl. "That, sounds great he said", before rotating his head on his neck to crack it into place for the day.
"Soooooo.... why am I in here? Have I done something wrong?"
"Oh no. No no, nothing wrong. In fact, I've got some rather good news for you."
"Oh yeah, what about?" she replied, genuinely curious.
"Well, we've been liaising with our partner company in the US," he said, "the one who sent you. You know? Providing feedback, sending through your numbers, letting them know how you've been getting on here in the UK."
"Right?"
"Right, yeah, so" stuttered Hardy. He had no problem addressing his power in front of his other office workers, but somehow, Tina had this confidence that annulled his authority. "So, obviously your numbers here speak for themselves, and we've been providing positive feedback of your progress and team mentality. Your US office have been passing these details to other branches within the

company that are looking for more senior members of the team, to, well, slot into managerial type roles."
Tina sat forward, and rested her head into her cupped hands that were joined together by the wrists.
"So, what does this all mean then?"
"Let me cut to the chase shall I?" asked Hardy, rhetorically.
Tina nodded.
"Tina, you have been offered a promotion within the company. A coordinator role in New York at one of the head offices. Your role will include teaching and mentoring new members of the team, using the experience you have drawn from working internationally within the company."
Tina was in shock. Excited nerves struck through her cerebrum and flashes of home, family, weather, dollar notes, yellow cabs, and busy lifestyle flickered like cars driving on the freeway. Her just sitting on a bench at the side, watching it all, not trying to stop it.
"So?" asked Hardy, "Sound, I don't know, promising?"
Tina gasped, "Yeah. Wow. I mean, that's a big decision to make. Back home. I mean, to New York City."
"Well, if it, helps. Your office will be on Madison Avenue, which is like, what do you guys say again, a "block" away from the Empire State. If you ask me, this is a job of a lifetime Tina. Of course, we'll be sad to see you go, but you're looking at a pay rise of at least 30% here, and accommodation at a reduced company rate. Flights included."
She was speechless. Hardy continued, "Thing is though, they have messaged me multiple times over the weekend, telling me to keep you informed about this from first thing Monday morning." Hardy clicked his pen a few times.
"I believe that there are other candidates in line who would jump at the opportunity."

Tina said she ought to get back to work, but that she would let him know her decision by the end of the day. She needed to speak to Dawn and most importantly, her mom.

Chapter 39

Mike called in sick on Monday morning. He was sick alright. Sick of having to explain himself to everyone. Sick of work, sick of Sharon, sick of Tina's messages, her coldness. He just couldn't handle going into the office that morning. So much so that he had set an alarm before going to bed, at a perfect time to let Mr Hardy know about his unexpected illness and how rough his night had been. There was no need for specifics. The only person who actually knew *all* the specifics was him. Sharon had moved to her sister's for a while, but she didn't really know the full extent of what had happened. He doubted she wanted to. Or maybe she did? 'God I miss her comfort' he thought.

He had pulled on a t-shirt, jumper and a pair of jeans after he actually awoke. He fell asleep for another two hours after his 07:20 email to the boss, so it was now around half nine and Mike wanted to get straight out of the house. He got in his car, wound the window down despite the frost in the air, and reversed his car off the driveway. He would go to the petrol station and fill up. Buy some fags whilst he was at it. As he drove down the chilly winter road, he thought back to when he and Sharon had moved in here. 'It must have been fifteen years ago at least', he thought. Families had changed during that time. Different sets of kids playing out on the road. First boys, then girls, then no-one. Not since technology had sucked them all up and kept them in the safety of their bedrooms. All that could be heard was the sound of his car engine, grumbling like a bitter old man. But Mike felt a loneliness, cutting right through him. A butchers knife through his liver. He felt like he had no one to turn to, except for probably Chris. But he really didn't want Chris to see him like this. All down and out. He turned the corner and saw the old lollipop lady by the zebra crossing. She stopped him to allow a mother to cross the road with a pram. It was a perfect pram, all traditional looking. Powder blue. It all came clearly to Mike then, whilst his car sat at the zebra crossing. He gazed through the front window, first at the smiling old lady in her yellow coat, then at the painted black and white stripes on the road. All he could think about was one thing. One real reason why all this had occurred. Sharon had always wanted a child with him, but he just couldn't bring himself to it. He couldn't be a father; or at least he couldn't be *the* father that he felt he needed to be.

There was a queue at the petrol station. A few cars lined up needing to fill themselves with juice. Upon checking his phone, he saw he had another message from Tina, asking him if he was coming into work today, and why he hadn't had the courtesy to reply to her messages. He ignored the message, and sat there patiently. His mind wandered off on another one of its tangents. He imagined he were some mob boss, controlling the petroleum industry. This particular station was owned by a rival of his, so he threatened the manager, smoked a cigarette, and flicked the burning butt at one of the tankers, walking away confidently from the grand explosion. He wasn't going to take any shit. He soon snapped out of his little daydream when the car in front of him set off. He pulled up to the petrol pump and got out, unscrewed the cap on his car, and began pumping petrol into the tank. It gurgled through the grey rubber pipe. His brain whirred to the noise of the pump. He thought of Tina. He thought of Sharon. Why is it, he thought, that you only ever think of the good stuff when things have failed. When things are going well, the good

things are blinded by further desires. He had no idea. He'd never been the best philosopher, and probably never would be. The sound of the petrol clicked, indicating he had a full tank, so he wandered over to the kiosk to be greeted by the usual attractive blonde.
"That's seventy-six eighty-two please"
Mike handed her his bank card.
"And a coupla packs of Marlboro as well please love"
"Sure, but we've only got Gold at the moment" she replied with a dainty smile.
"That'll do" he said.
She handed him the two packs, his card and his receipt, and then wished him a nice day. He could never tell if she was being genuine or not.

Despite the biting chill of the winter morning, a very soft peach sun poked through the faint clouds, overlooking the local park. It was a large park, with huge oak and birch trees deeply rooted. In the summer time there was so much colour here, so many beautiful shades of green. Mike didn't often come to the park, especially in winter when the branches were stark naked. But there was an appealing crunch underfoot, and there were no children as it was a school day. He walked, hands in pockets, wishing he had brought a scarf with him. The bitter cold was finding its way down his crew neck, infiltrating his insulation. He hadn't dressed prepared for the park, but he figured he hadn't been well prepared for anything that had occurred as of late. He took out a cigarette and lit it after a few attempts. He walked around the gravel pathway, staring at the light crystal frost which settled on the blades of grass. He smoked in silence, and avoided a few small dog turds which had been left on the path by lazy selfish owners. Mike had been selfish recently. He knew that much, but

rather than try and fight it, rather beat himself up about it, he chose instead to accept it.
'Everyone's selfish in their own little way' he thought. Agreeing with his self-justification. He heard a dog bark and peered into the distance. It wasn't a foggy day but there was a dewy mist in the air, caused from the warming of the frost by the overarching sun. The dog was sitting next to a bench, upon which sat its owner. As Mike got closer, he could distinguish that the dog was a black Great Dane. Sitting there like a gentle giant, not complaining about the cold. The owner must have been in his late sixties. Apparent from his white greasy ponytail and abundance of rings upon his fingers.
"How's it going there?" he said to Mike, in a low peaceful voice. "Sorry about Frank. He's got a loud bark he has. Always has done."
"Not to worry" said Mike, "It's a beautiful dog I must say"
"Well, thank ya sir. He's been my companion for over thirteen years now." The owner stroked Frank, giving Mike an extended view of all the copper and gold signet rings on his fingers. He wore an old brown leather jacket, which at one time, was lined with thick sheepskin. The remains of which still clung to the inside, but the white had discoloured to yellow.
"You got a dog yourself son?" he asked Mike, who took the opportunity to sit down on the bench beside the man.
"Yeah. Toby. He's......well, he's not very well at the moment"
"Poor thing. That's what most folk don't realise. A dog's not just for Christmas. They take a lot of looking after. Hence why I look like shit, and he's the most handsome devil in the world." He started to chuckle, and pet his dog some more. "Aren't ya boy. Aren't ya?" Mike smiled and watched

the dog enjoy the attention. It's eyes rolled back in ecstasy, every time the owner stroked slowly from its nose down its head.

"What's your name son?" the man asked, extending an open hand.

"Mike"

"Nice to meet ya Mike, I'm Leonard."

"Nice to meet you too. Mind if I smoke?"

"Do I look like the kinda guy who minds if you smoke?"

Mike laughed. "Not really".

Leonard pulled out a half smoked cigar from a tin which he kept in the inside pocket of his coat.

"Got a light?" he asked politely.

"Sure" replied Mike, before a moment of silence fell on the strangers. They pulled on their smokes, and Frank reshuffled his tail.

"So," said Leonard, looking out at the grass, "I've got to ask. What's a man like you doing alone at the park on a day like this?"

Mike was a little taken aback. "How come?" he replied, taking another drag from his cigarette.

"Well, I come to this park with this old pooch every Monday without fail. Usually, I see very few people here. Most folk are at work aren't they. So, I just wondered what your story was?"

Leonard was a curious soul, but he wasn't intrusive. His voice was calm, soft, accepting. His manner retired. Mike thought about lying to him, but then figured there was no point. He'd done enough lying and deceiving recently, and like Tina had told him, there was a level of trust you could get from a stranger, that a friend or family member could never offer.

"I called in sick" Mike said, looking down at the small stones on the ground.
Leonard waited a touch, then replied rather simply.
"You don't look sick." The breeze blew against Mike's vacant gaze. "Unless it's something mental? Folk always forget about mental illness. Just 'cause you can't see it don't mean it ain't there."
"No no. Let's just say I had an eventful weekend" said Mike, still conscious of completely opening up to this stranger.
"Oh aye? Let me guess. Women."
Mike laughed, and threw the butt of his cigarette on the ground, stamping it out with his foot.
"Bullseye. How did you know?"
"Oh Mike. That's the thing about men. We're simple folk. And a wise man once told me, the only time a man has the blues, is over a woman." He paused, stroked his beard and pondered on his next comments. "Let me tell you son, I've got more sad stories about love than you can care to hear. You married?"
"Just about"
Leonard guffawed, "Well if it makes you feel any better, I've had two failed marriages and, well, I'm still here. Still breathing."
The men continued to smoke, and Mike recounted his story to Leonard. From the moment of Tina's arrival, right up until the present.
"To put it bluntly, things are a disaster right now"
"Well. You could say that Mike. But honestly, from my experience, these things have a way of working themselves out. I lost myself to love once. Canadian she was. Tall, thin, blonde, beautiful. We were young and free, and more importantly, both on the same page. I couldn't believe my

luck at the time. Alexandra her name was. Oh Alex, she meant the world to me. And for a time, I to her. One day, when I fell ill and had to go to hospital, she wasn't there. Right when I needed her the most. She just--"
"Disappeared."
"Exactly" he sighed. "And, for a time, I was distraught. I couldn't understand why she had just vanished from my life. I couldn't cope without her. I still think of her to this day, sweet Alexandra.... but, time heals."
Mike didn't know what to say, he just agreed.
"Your problem, of course," continued Leonard, "is that you've got two women in your life. Your wife, and this Tina. All you need to do, is figure out which one you want to fight for. It's still in your hands".
"I wish it was that simple" replied Mike. Checking his phone once more.

Chapter 40

He messaged Sharon a carefully calculated message. Sympathetic, loaded with remorse, yet also hopeful of the future. He believed in a brightness behind the dark clouds that had emerged, and that optimism was gently delivered through his invitation to "sort dinner out tonight". He felt he just needed time, to sit and explain things to his wife, or not even explain things, just show some appreciation. He knew he had let her down, but it wasn't confirmed that this was indeed the end for them. He just needed a response from Sharon. Something positive, something to confirm she was listening. Something productive to begin repairs on the damage he had caused.

The PlayStation. The very console that Chris had used as leverage during his cry for financial help; lay still in Mike's car boot. Wrapped in a couple of old blankets and towels which had made a habitat of the dark, dusty boot. Mike figured it was finally time to go and drop it back off, as he climbed back into his car and began warming his hands up. It was freezing inside the car, so he cranked up the heat ventilation, and continued to rub his hands together and blow hot air into them. He wasn't in the mood for the radio. Despite the words of wisdom he had just received from Leonard, Mike didn't feel in the mood to do anything. He embraced the silence of his car whilst it heated up. Rarely did he just sit there in silence. He enjoyed having no immediate purpose, and didn't feel that usual sense of underlying guilt you get from phoning in sick to work. He concentrated on his breathing. The engine was still off but the keys were waiting in the ignition. As he started searching his soul, focusing on his presence inside the car on that cold Monday afternoon, his mind raced like

Scalextric. Thoughts passing and speeding by. He tried to ignore them, but the more he tried the more they came, and the more thoughts he became attached to, until he practically forgot what he was doing. So he opened his eyes, and turned the key in the ignition. It had been five to ten minutes he had spent in silence in his car, which had warmed itself up nicely. Still no reply from Sharon.

The curtains were drawn at Chris' place. All of them, including the front living room and both front bedrooms. 'How odd' thought Mike, before remembering that it was a weekday and that most folk were at work. But he didn't think that Chris had a job at the moment. Hence the financial trouble. He pulled the key out of the ignition and climbed out of his car. He shut the door and walked round to the back to open up the boot with the same key. The back window of his vehicle was still frosted over, now misty from the indoor heat. Mike unwrapped the towels, to reveal the black console, pad, and the cd wallet which contained the game. That attractive tattooed woman still stared back at him, blowing him a kiss. The same way she did the day he received it. That's when he remembered the note that Chris had left. If he wasn't in now, it would be quite fitting to drop it back off with a note also. He figured there was something charming about a note. A handwritten one anyway. Something about the personalised scrawl of pencil or biro that conquered a digital message. He grabbed the items and walked up the front path to Chris' place. He rang the doorbell and waited, but couldn't hear any movement from inside. So Mike wandered around the side of the house but it was just as silent and void of life as the front. He knocked on the back door but had already resigned to the fact that Chris simply wasn't at home. So he turned back round and head to his car, thinking about another appropriate time to drop it back off.

"Hello?" came a frail voice from over the fence. "Hello?" It was the next door neighbour, catching Mike by surprise.

"Oh, hi, erm....is Chris in?"

Mike knew the answer was no but it was customary to ask as it also explained his reasoning for being by the back door. He was no thief. The neighbour was an elderly lady with permed hair and a walking stick. Her hair was that colour which merges between grey and purple, that sometimes happens to old men and ladies. Her voice was so soft and gentle, but with an undertone of helplessness.

"I think I saw him go out earlier. He's been going out an awful lot these days. I know because he passes my front window on his bicycle." She stopped and looked as if she had forgotten something. Then she continued, "Are you a friend of his?"

"I am, and I just wanted to drop something off. He lent it to me some time back."

The old lady suddenly became rather excited.

"Oh, not to bother. I could help you if you like?"

She was so innocent, and it would have been so easy for Mike to tell her "no but thanks", but he didn't want to disappoint her so he said, "Oh yeah?"

"Of courrrse!" she said, elongating her r. "If you like you can leave it here and when he comes home I will give him a call and tell him to come and collect it."

"Oh I don't want to put you though any trouble madam" he said, lifting the package in his arms to indicate the size and weight of the thing.

"Not at all, come here love" she said, beckoning him to her front door.

Edith sat Mike down in the front living room and made him a cup of tea. Evidently, this was a big occasion in her day, perhaps even her week. From what Mike could make out, she lived a quiet and lonely existence in absence of her late great husband Albert.

"We were like chalk and cheese" she said, "but he was my rock."

An old black and white photo of a couple walking hand in hand by the pier sat next to her television set.

"Is that you two there?" asked Mike, pointing at it.

"Sure is" she said, sipping her tea with a shaky hand. "That was a long time ago, mind. We used to live by the sea before we moved here."

Mike was wondering what the hell he was doing sitting in this stranger's living room. This was the second conversation he had embarked on with a stranger that day. But he couldn't refuse her offer of a cup of tea, especially as he felt some sympathy towards her. He knew full well he would have to put up with her ramblings for a while, but she was such a pleasant old lady.

He took a gulp from his brew.

"Do you have a pen and piece of paper?" he asked.

"Sure do" she said, hoisting herself out from her chair.

"Oh, don't worry I can grab it. Where is it?"

"Just in the kitchen on top of the microwave" she said so sweetly.

The kitchen smelled of old onions and cat hair, and looked as though it could do with a deep clean. A square pad of green post-it notes sat on top of the microwave, just as Edith had said, and next to it a black biro. He wrote the message there and then.

Tried dropping this off earlier but you weren't in. Edith told me to leave it with her. Really enjoyed the game and I'll miss it. Be great to play a game together sometime soon. Don't worry about returning the 150. It's my pleasure. Mike

He slipped the note inside the plastic wallet next to the disc, listened to a few more of Edith's tales, and then thanked her very much.

"Thanks again for this Edith. I really appreciate you helping me out."

"Oh no problem at all Michael. I love to be of use. Drive safely out there, the roads must be slippy!"

"I will do" said Mike, closing the door behind him.

Chapter 41

With no contact from Sharon, Mike went to bed early and alone that night. He eventually managed to get a few solid hours in, but he'd be lying to himself if he said he slept well. The duvet was cold to the touch, the wind howled and there was no body heat to keep him warm. It took him ages to drift off, with those flitting thoughts refusing to leave him alone. Before he went to bed he had messaged Tina. He promised himself he wouldn't, but felt enraged at Sharon's refusal to reply to his nice message about cooking dinner. All he said to Tina was that he would be back at work in the morning and that he was sorry for all the confusion and chaos. In truth, he was excited to see her again, but he hid this truth behind a focus to get his marriage back on track.

He got up early that morning, earlier than usual. He sent a quick email to Hardy, informing him that he would be returning to work today and was starting to feel better. 'If he asks, it was a stomach bug' thought Mike, pouring himself a bowl of cereal and a hot cup of coffee. As he sat there, munching on the milk soaked corn and wheat pieces, his mind played a game of tennis. Tina versus Sharon. Sharon served the ball, hard and fast. She had purpose and reasoning, and refused to soften her shot. Tina returned the ball reluctantly, as if she didn't really want to play. Sharon hit back with a stern back hand which Tina was unable to reach.

'Oh Tina' thought Mike. 'Oh Sharon.' Never in his life had he had to deal with such a dilemma. Leonard had told him that it was still in his hands, but Mike struggled to believe that. It felt as though he were a juggler, with the power

shifting in and out of his hands with every throw into the air. Was he going mad?
'Maybe I need to go and see a therapist about this shit' he thought, scooping the last mouthful of his cereal into his mouth. He wandered back upstairs to complete the finishing touches of his morning. His phone was flashing on the bedside table, and he wondered who it could be. Possibly a reply from Hardy containing some wisecrack about getting back to business pronto. He was hoping it was Sharon, whom he imagined lolled on her sister's spare bed, finishing off her *Pride & Prejudice & Zombies.* It wasn't either of them, it was Kevin.

Hi mate, hope you're feeling okay. Haven't heard from you since you left my pig sty. Hope you are back today to help regain my sanity. Kev

Mike chuckled, sent a quick reply, and sorted out his tie. He applied a little texturising gum to his hair, and squirted some after shave. On the surface, he felt better but in his heart, he still felt like a crumbled piece of paper which had been tossed in the bin.
As he opened the front door to go and get in his car, he saw that it had completely iced over during the night. Tiny hail stones remained on his driveway, like empty shells strewn on the battlefield. He kept his ice-scraper in the front glove box, so after some trying he managed to carve open the passenger side door and retrieve the manky yellow plastic scraper. He turned the engine on and set the heater to attack the windows, but the scraper was proving useless. He put some elbow grease into it, but it had layered on during the night and he figured he could be there twenty minutes scraping and it still wouldn't be fit to drive. So he wandered

back into the house and flicked the kettle on. Cautious as for the water not to fully boil. He didn't want to completely crack the glass. After a couple of back and forth trips with the warm kettle water, his car was ready to take him to work.

Mike arrived to the work carpark on time and didn't struggle to find a spot. The sky was a tinted purple colour and it was drizzling. He felt strange due to his fake illness and lack of contact with Tina, but he was sure these feelings would pass once he'd got the first working hour out of the way. He didn't look like shit, but inside he felt like a bankrupt gambling addict. As he took the lift up to the thirteenth floor, he hummed a common Christmas tune, and considered how he would pass Christmas Day this year, now that his life had been thrown into the air. He had very little affection left for his job now, and if it wasn't for Kevin and Tina, he would seriously consider packing it in and looking for something new. Something that could prove difficult with the same company on his CV for the last twenty odd years. The lift pinged and the silver doors repelled each other. An unexpected sound of soft jazz music played on the office floor. Something Mike had never heard once in his time on floor thirteen.

'Perhaps Hardy is finally cracking up' he thought, smiling inside his head. But there was more strangeness about the day.

"Morning Mike" said Babs, whose workstation was in immediate eyeshot of the lift.

"How are ya feeling?" asked Carol, who always had that caring, mothering side to her.

"Morning Babs, morning Carol," he said, before lying, "Much better actually, thanks for asking."

Tina and Ian's desks were vacant, but Kevin sat at his computer as always, typing away with his headset on. It was nice for Mike to see a friendly face.
"Morning Mike! Nice to see you back" he said, removing his headset.
"Nice to see you too mate" replied Mike, dusting off his monitor and keyboard, "What's with all the music?"
"I'm not entirely sure why there's jazz music playing" said Kevin, "but there are some changes happening in the office that I'm sure you're soon to find out about."
"Oh aye? Changes?" said Mike, a little puzzled, sitting down in his chair and glancing up at Mr Hardy's office. Ian was in there, nodding his head to the tune of Hardy's voice like a lovesick puppy.
"Apparently" replied Kev.
"Where's Tina?" asked Mike, before she appeared from the kitchen holding a cakebox in her hands. She was wearing her usual work attire. Pencil skirt, frilled white shirt and a charcoal grey blazer, but she had done something with her hair. Pinned it up in some style which resembled a celebrity in Sharon’s magazine. Her eyes met with Mike's from across the room, and in a moment of slowed motion, her large smile faded. She must have known from his innocent wide eyes that he had no idea.
'What on earth is going on?' he thought, as Tina went from desk to desk, delivering her fancy cupcakes. She moved to the sound of the jazz, so smoothly across the office floor. Mike's mind automatically shut out all other sounds, including the babble from Babs, the graciousness of Carol and the overdramatic thanks from Ian who had emerged from Hardy's office with a big grin on his face. She arrived at Mike's desk and he interpreted the words from her lips.
"Come with me, we need to talk"

Mike hadn't asked for Hardy's permission to take a cigarette break, but time was of the essence and his burning desire to know what was going on took him straight to the lift. The small confines of the lift, alongside the mirrors, gave the effect of claustrophobia.
"Babs will probably snitch on me" he said to Tina in the lift, whom he was struggling to look fully in the eye.
"Maybe" she said, before the silence of the lift held the conversation. In both their heads, they played out the conversation in every detail they had imagined.
"Look" said Mike, "I'm really sorry that I left you at the hotel. It's just-"
"Don't" said Tina, as the pair descended towards the ground floor, "You don't need to tell me all the details. I know you're feeling apologetic and that's all that matters."
The humming of the lift's machinery was all that could be heard, until the doors opened.
"And I'm sorry I didn't reply to your messages. It's been, well, it's been a difficult time for me, and, I-"
"You're forgiven" she said, smiling that smile and offering him a Camel cigarette.
They buttoned up their jackets and sat down outside in the same place they had sat those weeks ago when they first got to know each other. Tina sparked them both up.
"So?" suggested Mike.
"So, what?"
"Oh come on Tina, you know what. The jazz music, the cupcakes. What the hell is going on?" He aggressively exhaled the smoke from his first drag.
Tina looked at him, in a way that reminded him of Toby. Open-eyed, almost sorrowful. A single tear ran down her cheek, culminating at her precious freckle.
"Well"

"Well what?" demanded Mike, whose impatience had grown to a degree of anger.

Tina decided not to beat around the bush any longer. She knew it would upset Mike, and she herself felt some sadness at leaving him. The rain continued to drizzle down on them.

"I'm leaving"

"Leaving? The company?"

"No, the country."

"Why?"

"I've been offered a dream position in New York City. I'd be a fool to refuse it Mike."

She was the iceberg to his titanic. His whole body sunk as the ice-cold sharpness punctured what was left of him. He said nothing, so she continued.

"I'm sorry Mike. I know we were just getting to know one another, and, I must admit some feelings for you had begun to grow-"

"Stop." he said, "I don't want to know, it only makes this harder."

She smiled sympathy towards him. He wasn't one to show his emotions, but he could feel the bubble growing inside of him. He tried his hardest to contain it but it burst, resulting in tears of shame, disappointment and sheer loneliness. Nothing could be heard but the pattering of the rain, the low cries of the wind, and the occasional sniffle from his nose. He wiped his tears away and said,

"So this is your last day?"

She nodded, and looked at the ground where a damp pile of her cigarette ash lay.

"When do you fly?"

"Tomorrow"

"Will you stay in touch?" he asked in anguish.

"Only if you want to" she replied in atonement.

Tunnel Vision

Good evening Michael, how are you? I received your letter. Care to explain?

Evening Doc. Yeah, about that. I just feel like it's time for me to move on from this. I've poured out more feelings to you than I've poured myself drinks, and well, you know, it feels like the right time for me to stop coming.

Of course, if you feel the time has come to stop attending these sessions, I accept and respect your decision. As your therapist I must say that I think it may be too soon, but really, only you know that.

Right. I thought you might say that. And who knows? I might be back in this chair before you know it. But I've taken on board you're advice, and I think it might be time for me to start dealing with the consequences of my actions, well, on my own.

So, you feel you've learnt something here?

Oh sure. Sure I have Doc. And god knows, I'm hardly the easiest client you've had to deal with.

You're a unique one Michael, I must admit. But, seriously, you wouldn't believe the amount of characters I've had the pleasure of working with.

God bless client confidentiality hey. But yeah, listen here, there's one last story I need to tell you about. But as always, you mustn't judge.

I'm all ears Michael.

Ever the listener… well, it all took place out in the desert. There's this sandy town in the north west where the cars are all rusted, the coyote's howl and the hillbillies drink each other's piss. All that weird crap. Well, let me tell you Doc, Methamphetamine is a big problem.

I read about this in the news.

Yup. Well, I was out there drinking a few beers at a bar. A tipoff had told me that a major crank deal was going down, and asked if I would be able to be there, just to keep an eye on things. Most people don't know me up there so it's easy for me to keep a low profile. I didn't mind, so long as it paid right, and besides, most of these meth heads don't know shit except for crystal. To put it bluntly, these guys aren't the sharpest tools in the yard.

I see. Although, I've heard they can be somewhat, unpredictable.

Oh sure. When they are on the crank, it fucks with their mind and sends them into this rage of paranoia. When they aren't on it, that's all they focus on. Trying to get on it. But that's beside the point. There was this major meet going down between two large distributors. One party were supposed to be arriving in four-by-fours and the other party were due to arrive on a freight train from the city. I knew the train wasn't due to arrive until gone ten, and so I waited in a nearby saloon, sipping on a few cold ones, biding my time. I sat alone by a small window, so that I could see the arrival of the vehicles. I phoned my tipoff back, just to double check things were running smoothly, and he assured me that the four-by-fours would arrive first, and that I was sitting in the perfect vantage point. I had a satchel with me, which contained the various parts of an M4 carbine rifle. I'd even packed the added extras including a rubber grip, extra magazines, a scope and a detachable under-mount grenade launcher.

Oh gosh. That sounds like a serious piece of kit. What were you expecting to happen?

I mean Doc, in that sort of situation you really can't afford half measures. These particular parties are two of the largest meth distributors in the state, and well, lets just say they don't fuck about. Besides the fact that I was getting paid a hefty sum, and hefty sums don't come for no reason. There had been friction between these two parties in the past. Nothing I had ever dealt with directly, but certainly stuff I had heard about during my time here.

Right.

Right. So, there I am twiddling my thumbs, sipping on another beer. When I see through the window two large Humvees arrive, along with a coupla motorcycles. They pulled up on the other side of the train tracks, and arrived at some speed. The guys inside the black Humvee's remained inside, and the motorcyclists got off, removed their helmets and leaned against their bikes, having a smoke. I had a second hand car with me, parked out front. Rusty old thing, but that's what I needed to fit in with my surroundings. I had no idea what to expect, but I had been told to keep my wits about me. To be ready for anything.

I see. So now, all parties, including yourself, were waiting for the train to arrive?

Exactly. I finished off my beer, picked up my satchel and went and sat in the front seat of my car. It was dark, so nobody could see me attaching the various parts of the gun together. The barrel was as clean as a whistle, and I'd made sure the serial number had been removed. It's weird, on the one hand I wanted this deal to run smoothly, but on the other hand I was anticipating some action. I had that buzz that comes with a job like this one. I attached the scope and the grip, but left the grenade launcher in the bag. I got a message on my phone that read, 'It's on', and that's when I heard the loud sound of the train. It hissed and horned and chugged down the tracks, right towards the remote desert station. I fired up my engine and drove a little closer to the tracks, parking up by a few construction vehicles and a large billboard. This billboard had a long ladder stretching up to it, so I climbed it to get a perfect height advantage over the deal. My tipoff had asked me to try and get some photos, so I brought a small yet powerful camera with me in my satchel. I remember the sounds of the train getting louder and louder as I climbed up that cold, metal ladder. I took my position up there, and watched as a group of about ten men jumped from off the freight train, all of 'em packing heat. The pictures I gotta say, turned out a little blurry. I was fuckin' nervous up there with that wind. I snapped what I could, then watched as the two bikers walked towards the back of the Humvees. Assumably to pick up the product. I could feel the bite of the tension. I zoomed in with my scope and saw some kinda comms device. The two bikers pressed it and hell started to break loose as a couple of helicopters came heading over the mountain top. The guys that had got off the train opened fire, and I was under order to eliminate on sight if the deal got out of hand. I took shots at the guys who came by vehicle, but the choppers were incoming fast. So I slid down the ladder and chased the shadows up to the train, which had restarted it's engine and was about to head back the way it had come from. Back towards the city.

Oh my, I mean. Oh my, are you serious?

Deadly. A few of the train gang had managed to jump back on board the train and I had no option other than to board it also. It was either that, or back to the rust bucket I had used as a decoy at the saloon. These helicopters, they weren't police. And they weren't army. I'm talking blacked out assault choppers with mounted shit all over them. This deal had got to be the biggest explosion of artillery I've happened to find myself upon, *this side* of the border.

Ha!

No, I'm serious Doc. This was some serious shit. Bullets flying everywhere, the train started to go full steam ahead back on its tracks. I was held onto the side still facing the saloon as I watched it fade away in the distance. I managed to take out a few of the dealers who were clambering up the train to try and get to the top, assuming there was a hatch up there. Yeah, and then I made my way up there too and attached my under-mount RPG. The train was heading fast towards a tunnel so I fired a few grenades and heard the gulp of the gun which jolted me back. I had to fall flat on my face and grip the roof as I escaped the scene, breathing wildly as we vanished into the tunnel.

Chapter 42

Within a week or two of her leaving, the divorce papers had come through. Aside from one angry phone conversation, Mike had not seen or spoken to Sharon, and Sharon hadn't been to the house once. Steph had been sent over one evening to collect some of her sisters clothes and bits and bobs, but had refused to give anything away to the desperate and broken Mike.

"Please, can you just ask her to see me!?" he begged, standing at the foot of the stairs.

"I can't" said Steph, overwhelmed with pain. She was stomping around upstairs collecting hand towels and make-up.

"Why?"

"Because..." said Steph, in that way that doesn't really answer anything. Just as she had been gathering the last of the things on her list, she said, "Mike?"

"What?"

"Can I ask you, have you heard from him?"

"Him? You mean Richie?”

"No. Tony.”

"No, nothing. Why? What happened."

Steph snapped back to reality. She got what she needed.

"Why the fuck should I tell you? You've left my sister with no choice also! Same as him."

There weren't too many more words exchanged between the two on that frosty occasion.

The house felt cold. No Sharon, no Toby; just Mike and Chris, who sat in the living room together. Mike in his worn-leather chair, Chris cross-legged on the floor. Mike glared right through him. Like he wasn't even there. An ethereal being.

"What happened Mike?" asked Chris, concerned.
Mike grunted something he couldn't make out. Then shook his eyes and wiped them with his thumb and forefinger, like that eyestrain reaction from too much screen staring.
"Has she left?"
"Who? Shaz?"
“Yeah."
"Apparently. Well, I think most definitely, the divorce papers are upstairs on the bedside table."
Chris was frozen. He could feel the shock of it all rush through his body. Somehow, he felt a level of guilt.
"Divorce? My god I had no idea Mike. I'm so sorry...."
Mike changed his attitude, which as of late had been up and down like a yo-yo. He was toying with the idea of how his new future might be.
"Don't be. What's happened has happened. I don't really want to go into too much detail, but there was," he thought of Tina, walking confidently out of Saks on fifth avenue, "there was another woman involved."
Chris was curious, but aware of being too intrusive.
"Oh? You mean, someone serious, or, or, just a one night kinda thing?"
Mike pondered the question, and rubbed the dark stubble of his chin.
"I'm not sure."
The truth was, that Mike had probably been spending more time thinking about Tina than he had his soon to be ex-wife. He felt deeply saddened that his marriage had failed, and still wished that Sharon hadn't found out anything about Tina. That thought crossed his mind aplenty. But when he started to think more objectively about the whole situation, it was Tina who re-sparked that fire in his belly. The belly of the beast. Mike couldn't see much of a future

with Sharon, especially now it had gone past the point of no return with the whole children idea. He had been spending hours, even days sitting in his leather chair, smoking cigarettes and trying to intellectualise the reason why he had never succumbed to the idea of trying for a baby with Sharon. Was it that he didn't want children? Was it that a child would add to his sense of entrapment? Or was it just the wrong woman? Had he fallen out of love with Sharon a long time ago? Is that the reason why he had been led astray by his attractive North American ex-colleague? It didn't even matter to him now, and all the thoughts he could possibly have about the situation, had already been had, evaluated and dissected.

"Anyway, enough about me. How about you? How are you doing matey?" he asked, animating himself.

Chris smiled with joy, before becoming conscious of appearing too happy in front of his broken childhood friend.

"Yeah. Things are, well, pretty great to be honest. But I feel kinda bad talking about it when you're feeling...."

"Nah fuck that" said Mike, genuinely interested in Chris' story. "Go on!"

"Well, when I contacted you, you know, about the money."

"Yeah"

"Well I was pretty low. I wasn't financially stable and I had sunk into a level of what most people would call depression."

The word impacted like a single bullet from a rifle.

“It got to the point where I really needed to do something about it. I needed a job, first and foremost. You know I dropped out of school early, and at the time it didn’t really matter to me. I got on that apprenticeship at the fish factory

and the money was coming in. But there's only so far that can take you, you know?"
Mike nodded. It felt good to listen to someone else. He was aware that he'd been so tied up in his own problems.
"I mean, there are only so many jobs you can get without any qualifications. So, not long after we went for those drinks at the pub, I enrolled myself at night college. Ha! I know, I must be the oldest student in the world, but I'm enjoying my course, and I just got myself a new part-time job in the warehouse at that new supermarket that opened up by the shopping centre. It's a stopping gap for sure, but being productive is helping with my positivity."
A slight of jealousy crept under Mike's skin. He felt awkward about it. He knew he should be happy for Chris, but he never thought he would be envious of his positive attitude.
"Did you end up finding a therapist in the end? I remember you mentioned it at the Bull's."
Chris laughed, "Nah, not yet. The public mental health service has a massive backlog, and well, ya know I can't afford a private one. But guess what?"
"What? You've got a girlfriend?" guessed Mike.
Chris smiled. It was one of those uncontrollable smiles which only appear from infatuation. Mike smiled back at him.
"You're back with Victoria?"
"Nah, not quite. But me and her have kept in touch, as friends like.
"Ahh that's good" said Mike, thinking of Shaz.
"But yeah, I met someone new."
"Oh yeah?"

Chris beamed, "Yeah. Kate she's called. I met her on the open evening for college and we just, well, hit it off I guess you could say."
Mike sunk into deep thought, and Chris noticed it. So he purposely steered the conversation.
"I brought the PlayStation over in case you fancied a game of something. I'm borrowing another pad from our kid brother. It's just in my bag in the hall, I've got a few games we can choose from."
"Yeah, sounds good mate" answered Mike.
Chris wandered into the hall to go and unpack the console. Mike thought about the divorce papers, and how much the whole saga was going to cost him. He thought of the money he had earned, and how he didn't want to use that on a lawyer and all that stuff. No, he wanted to use it on a holiday. He needed one now. He looked out the window at the trees shaking in the wind. Then imagined himself boarding a transatlantic flight to JFK. It was certainly possible. He snapped out of it when Chris re-entered the living room. Mike looked up at his mate, cradling the console and cables in his arms.
"Shall I put the kettle on?"

***

Epilogue

The whole journey he had been alone. Twisting and turning through dark tunnels, into the unexpected. At first he'd felt that mixture of nerves and excitement. Deep in the pit of his stomach. It was cold down here. In and amongst the roots of this concrete jungle. The feelings were so real, but everything else so fake, so plastic. The carriage hadn't stopped once, and as he got out of another seat and peered back through the transparent windows, he could feel the darkness lighten. He knew these tracks wouldn't continue forever. The motion of the wheels had been so steady on this journey, and whilst he continued to worry about the next chapter, the next life form to enter, he remembered the woman. She too remained alone, a few carriages down, still reading. He wondered if she could see him, gazing at her from a distance. As the train took an abrupt left, screeching round the bend, she glanced at her watch. She was aware of the time, but he wasn't. He had no timekeeper, no idea of when it would stop. It was then that everything ground to a halt. The piercing shriek of metallic so obtrusively loud. So painful. The darkness outside lightened, and the doors slid open. He wondered whether he should get off, when all of a sudden the sound of running footsteps overpowered everything. A third person was about to board the train. It was a man, tall and dark. He was heading to a carriage towards the woman, and just made it on board before the doors closed again. Staring through the windows he saw the woman put down her book, smile, stand up and greet the newcomer. It was her, and she embraced the new man like a lover.

Printed in Great Britain
by Amazon